MILESTONES & MILLSTONES

MARK HURST

DEDICATION

This book began as a single Post-it note. Then another. Then another. Like a couple of other nonfiction books I've written, it is a casual, unintentional, collection of various notes and scraps of paper on which I would scribble a few words as a reminder of a thought or an experience I've had, maybe an observation or two of the smallest of things going on around me. Small things, I've learned, can make a big difference in how we see ourselves and how we see others.

In order to weave it all into a book, it took hundreds of hours of digging, deciphering, and decoding, during a time in my life of extreme hardship and inner turmoil unlike any other I have known. In order to do that I've relied on the strength of my wife and family who see my daily struggles, my meltdowns, my crashes and then carry me on their shoulders. They are amazing people, and I thank them. I love them. This is for you.

INTRODUCTION

Today's interstate freeways are dotted with green mile markers, nearly inconspicuous little signs that vanish into the background. We don't pay them much attention until we run out of gas, have a flat tire or an accident. Then we can let someone know where we are if we need help.

Anciently, the Romans built their version of markers from stone, placing them along the famous Appian way and the other phenomenal roads they built throughout their vast empire. I've seen a few of the markers in England where they are listed as "historically significant," and are protected by the government. Travelers in ancient Rome knew how far they had come in their journey and how far they still had to go. They are **milestones**.

Change one letter and the word "**milestone**" becomes "**millstone**."

Our ancestors devised a way to grind wheat by harnessing a horse or an ox to a yoke which would turn gears attached to a very large round, stone, pulverizing the wheat into flour. These are known as **millstones**.

Today we use the phrase "a millstone hung around your neck" to describe the heavy burdens we carry around. Many of them we have hung there ourselves, (bitterness, jealousy, envy, and self-loathing); many have been placed there by others, (harsh criticism, gossip, resentment, abandonment, broken human connections); and some of these weighty, giant stones that are pulverizing you are the result of things beyond your control (sickness, disease, trauma, grief, mental and physical limitations.)

At first glance, these two words, **milestones** and **millstones**, look identical. A change of just one letter gives you two completely different words, a complete opposite from the other. It suggests that with the simplest of solutions, we can begin changing ourselves, our outlook and our relationships.

I let this curious, little grammatical oddity guide me through my woolgathering, collecting stories, observations, and a few deeply personal experiences from my life that have inspired me, informed me, or at the very least given me something to think about in new ways.

The entire book is focused on joy, where to look for it, and how to live a life full of happiness, inner peace and strength, regardless of your out-of-control-poundage.

Each chapter, each story is meant to suggest that weighty millstones can be removed, and that new milestones will come into view, guiding you, moving you forward in your search for a more fulfilling life.

I've laid bare my soul here, perhaps a bit too personal for some. My intent was never to talk about me, rather to point out markers I've observed that line my personal pathway to joy as I set about breaking apart a couple of significant millstones I'm packing around.

Woven into these diverse, quirky, open-book cogitations, are very specific ways you can seize control of your brain and train it help you find joy, no matter what.

My hope is that one or two little nuggets of my meandering musings, will resonate with you, perhaps even inspire you and help you take an important first step, then another, then another, focused on your end goals, confident of your pace.

THE AUTHOR

TABLE OF CONTENTS

"TOMORROW IS
THE FIRST BLANK PAGE
OF A 365-PAGE BOOK.
WRITE A GOOD ONE."

BRAD PAISLEY

1

PAINTING BARNS

In 2019 we all learned about the Corona virus, witnessing its rapid spread around the globe, watching the news, watching health-care officials and the government bungle everything about it. I contracted COVID and, thankfully, made it through without serious symptoms, the worst being the lingering smell of burning tires mixed with stale Thanksgiving stuffing, the disgusting fragrance of rubber and sage.

Right in the middle of the mess, I was diagnosed with Parkinson's disease. It was puzzling at first that, just like COVID, the medical community has never fully understood Parkinson's. It has been around for hundreds of years, and still we are told there is no cure, no prevention, no known cause, and no way to even test for it. You just get it, like waking up in the morning with all that crusty stuff deposited in the corners of your eyes.

It just shows up.

My neurologist did an evaluation, then looked me in the eye and proceeded to hang a giant millstone around my neck. I gave up golf, followed by flyfishing, wood carving, gardening, foreign travel and other things I've always been able to do. Every aspect of my life ground to a halt and I gave my life over to prescription drugs. I had to decide if the millstone was going to permanently pummel me or if I could find challenges, joy, satisfaction and personal growth in other ways.

One morning I sat down at my computer and began writing a novel. It's a work of historic fiction that recounts experiences of my grandfather who survived the Great Depression by shearing sheep in the Yellowstone Wilderness area. No, I'd never written a novel before. I had no idea about character development, story arcs, conflict and resolutio, and the art of storytelling. The first draft was horrible. The second draft not much better. Then after an additional eight complete rewrites, and some advice from a historic fiction consultant, I felt like I had a story worthy of my grandfather's amazing accomplishments. If I hadn't written a good book, I had at least made an unforgettable connection with history and a grandfather I loved.

Writing became my therapy, my security blanket.

I wrote two nonfiction books as well, and I am continuing to write despite stiff fingers and shaky hands that struggle to make their way around the keyboard. None of the books are runaway bestsellers. I never supposed they would be. I'm certainly no Steinbeck. But I wrote and published three books. I say this with no intent to boast, only to point out that words became my chisel, books a hammer that helped me break apart my giant millstone, confident that others can find the resolve, the right tools, and the strength to smash and destroy their personal millstones.

Still, I wanted other challenges. I wanted other outlets for my creative energy. I was not going to let Parkinson's park me, beat me or defeat me. My disease is degenerative, but it doesn't mean my attitude has to be.

I took up watercolor painting. Artists of all types told me that it's the hardest of all techniques, difficult to control, impossible to master. It would require a steady hand which, in my case, was anything but.

10

All I kept hearing was, "Persons with Parkinson's don't paint." I have a very large stack of failures in a cupboard, probably around one hundred or more, and as I look back on them, I realize the experts were right. It is very, very frustrating. But as I gradually learned how to mix colors and control the random flow of water, I began to make progress. I'm still very much in the beginner phase but I am making progress. And that is my goal, keep making progress.

As I looked around for subjects I could paint, I found reference photos of places where I have travelled, some from my own files, others sourced from internet searches.

One afternoon I stood on my front porch, admiring the views of our stunning community, Cache Valley in northern Utah. Just across the way I could see a historic, red barn, probably around 120 years old. An artist's dream. "Why am I painting landscapes in Europe when I have magnificent subjects to choose from right here in my own front yard," I mused.

I walked over to the farmyard of my neighbor who owned the barn and found no one home. I strolled around the dirt road, peeked in the windows of a couple of out-buildings, circumnavigated two grain silos, imagining early settlers building and running a farm, making a living from the land. I took twenty or thirty pictures of the barn, looking for just the right angle.

I immediately went back to my little studio, opened the photos on my computer, made a few tweaks to the composition, and went to work. My first barn. It was my first real success, at least I thought so.

Forty-eight hours later the barn burned to the ground. A rogue ember from a small fire landed on the very old, very dry, very vulnerable roof and set off a blaze that could not have been faster and more destructive if an atomic bomb had hit it. In just minutes, the structure was completely engulfed in flames and made a roar you could hear miles away.

Fire trucks arrived but could only douse the pile of rubble. There was nothing to save. Where there was, just a few moments earlier, a stately architectural masterpiece, now, just a heap of black dreck, muddy from the spray, ashes in the air, and an acrid stench in your nostrils.

For the next weeks and months, I painted images of twenty-three historic structures here in our very small farming community. I fell in love with barns. I've painted dozens of them and keep finding new images from all over North America and Europe. I'm an accidental painter of barns, relics, history, and stories they tell, stored in now empty hay lofts and feeding stalls.

On the hillside, just a few moments from my home, is one other barn, one of the saddest subjects I came across. It's hard to say why it's still standing. Already leaning, lurching and falling apart, it is, sadly, on its last legs, and took a cruel beating from the worst Utah winter on record. Any number of artists have painted it in its current state, dilapidated, no life support in sight, large gaping holes that expose the skeletal structure inside. It's more holes than barn, more air than wood, bony, gaunt, tragic.

I chose to not paint it in its dilapidated state. I let my imagination fill in all the missing boards, let my eyes see what it had been, not what it is. A reminder, not a remainder. I restored it to its original splendor. (Now that is really a stretch for an amateur painter, barely six months into my experimental hobby. I couldn't possibly restore its splendor, but, in my simple way I tried putting it back together.) I love the results. Mrs. Hawkes, who owns the barn seemed pleased as well.

It will be gone soon, joining thousands of other barns lost

to the harsh elements, the maelstrom of modernity, timber giving way to cheap aluminum and steel, utilitarian, functional, but ugly and cold.

I'm not a great painter. I'm not a great writer. I'm neither architect nor historian. But my attempts at capturing fleeting glimpses of history, restoring buildings that are broken, has restored and mended me. Invigorated me. I am stronger, for having tried. A rogue ember may be lurking somewhere, hoping to set my personal roof ablaze, but I'm having none of that. I'm watching for embers. I'm no Winslow Homer but I am making progress. And that is my goal: keep making progress.

I keep painting, good or bad, content to remain a student, content with all I'm learning about light and shadow, and especially perspective, seeing things in a new light, remembering that it is always light that defines the shadows. **MARK**

"THE SECRET TO SO MANY
ARTISTS LIVING SO LONG IS THAT
EVERY PAINTING IS A NEW
ADVENTURE. SO YOU SEE, THEY'RE
ALWAYS LOOKING AHEAD.
THE SECRET IS TO
NOT LOOK BACK."

NORMAN ROCKWELL

2

STIRRING THE NEST

It is the very last day of April, 2023, and the worst, the wettest, the wildest winter ever recorded in Utah has, mercifully, come to an end. Once again, I am intrigued by the springtime return of two hawks to a large cottonwood tree just outside my bedroom window. I've lived in a rural community for the past eight years and have enjoyed my neighbors: Mule deer, elk, skunks, at least one moose, racoons, wild turkeys and a host of other friends and foes. We have experienced a genuine Moses-like plague of frogs, hundreds of them in our window wells, flower beds, and just about everywhere on our acreage.

You can't predict when you'll see any or all of this odd menagerie, skittish as they are, but they hover around the edges of the land that, for hundreds of years, was theirs. We're the interlopers. We're the invasive species.

But, you can set your clock by the hawks. They return from their winter homes every March, and begin gathering sticks, straw, grass, and twigs to refresh the same nest that has been their permanent address for many years. At least for the last eight.

Officially, this bird of prey, a red-tailed hawk if I've researched it correctly, will typically live around 11-12 years in the wild, up to twenty-plus years in captivity. It is highly likely that

It's the same two birds each year, scientists telling us that they are, for the most part, monogamous. They mate while in the air, a ridiculous notion to those of us whose feet are permanently nailed to terra firma. And it should be noted that the female may occasionally kill the male if he doesn't bring around enough food to eat. I shall not comment further on this little scientific bit of information, tempted as I am to be cheeky.

While there are abundant hawks throughout the area we call Cache Valley, it is not often that we see the magnificent American bald eagle. But now and then they stop by, hang around for a few days, then head elsewhere. They could easily pick up one of our chickens for supper, and we fret about one day seeing our miniature Schnauzer, all nine pounds of him, being carried away in the enormous talons of *Haliaeetus Leucocephalus*.

The nests of the bald eagle are the largest of any bird in North America, typically in the range of 10-12 feet deep and 8 feet across. In zoological terms the nests are referred to as "Aeries". One nest can last up to five years, but scientists discovered one nest in the Midwest that was occupied continuously for thirty-four years. (Quick note: Aerie is a fantastic word when you have a tray full of vowels in *Scrabble*.)

I'm just an observer of all things avian, not an ornithologist, not a scientist, and I am not an expert on any of it. But I spent some time, recently, researching eagles to better respond to a neighbor who, by the look in her eye, seemed to doubt a comment I made to her. I don't think she ever used the word "liar," but she seemed skeptical. I don't want to embarrass her, so we'll keep her actual name confidential. Let's just call her Stephanie Wallis. Her son mows and edges my expansive lawn and has done so for the last three years. We were chatting about his schedule and settling on a weekly fee.

With negotiations concluded, I commented on Stephanie's kids, eight in all, and what a great bunch of kids they've turned out to be, remarkable in so many ways. Both Stephanie and her husband (for privacy sake we won't' use his real name and we'll just call him Brent Wallis,) thanked me for the compliment, then looked at each other with what I will call a tired smile, a quick, little, polite chuckle, followed by a nearly imperceptible twitching of an eye, a clenching of the jaw, considerable head-bobbing, and a down turning of a lower lip, eyes rolled upward, heavy blinking, all well-known indicators of fatigue, angst, worry, and all the other stressors that come with raising eight children. They both went on a meandering conversation that ranged from how much they truly love and cherish each child, to an unmistakable "can't wait to get them out of the house" attitude fueled by the challenge of feeding and clothing a very large family in the age of record inflation, educating them, and the struggles with maintaining order and discipline in a large family.

Two of the eldest Wallis kids, a son and a daughter are both off to new adventures and Brent and Stephanie (not their real names,) were clearly giddy about reducing head count. It was at this point that our conversation, oddly, turned to eagles.

I told them that I had, like Cliff Claven or a *Jeopardy* champion, discovered, somewhere over the years, the trivial, little-known fact that those giant nests of the bald eagles have a unique design element. During original construction, and yearly remodeling, mother and father eagle put, into the floor of the nest, sharp sticks, thorns, and a variety of other things, found at the Avian Home Depot, that are prickly, pointy, uncomfortable, and annoying. Tender hatchlings don't feel the prickliness at first because the nest has also been lined with feathers, dried grasses, and a soft lining to make the babies warm and comfortable. At about three weeks, momma eagle begins stirring the nest.

Humans have known about "stirring the nest" for hundreds of years. This from the Bible: *"Like an eagle that stirs up its nest and hovers over its young, that spreads its wings to catch them and carries them on its pinions."* Deut. 32:11

Feather by feather, Momma eagle begins removing the soft, protective wall to wall carpet, exposing the razor-sharp spikes. The babies keep getting bigger, the nest becomes more crowded and uncomfortable. It's time for the babies to fly. The father is tired of feeding them, and momma wants them gone, wants them to get a job, start their own family. Home is meant to be a very temporary shelter, not a lifetime sanctuary.

The eaglets begin easing up to the top of the nest, then perch on the edges where they see their environment for the first time. Sitting there, enjoying an Aerie reverie, figuring out what is to become of them, momma sneaks up from behind and does a very unmotherly thing. She gives them a shove.

Can you imagine thatr? A mother tossing her babies off the roof? They have no idea how to fly. They have no idea that they even have wings, much less, how they work. They have no idea they were endowed with the gift of flight, the power to soar.

They plummet to earth, a free-fall, no parachute. Their short lives appear to be over. Except that Momma swoops down, underneath them and catches them on her back. She then catches an updraft, warm spring air rising off the valley floor, soars to an even greater height, and, thoughtlessly, cruelly, dumps them off. After two or three trips on this amusement park ride from hell the young birds make an important discovery: "I better start flapping." In just a few short minutes they have left the nest and will never go back.

The home of the bald eagle is meant to be uncomfortable. In our homes, our human aeries, we make them cozy, comfortable, with free food every day, soft beds, fluffy pillows, electronics, phones, and entertainment on demand.

And WiFi. Gotta have that!

No wonder children, in increasing numbers are staying home. Or moving back in. Why would they ever leave?

The best thing we can do for our children: Kick them out. Push them off the edge. Prepare them to leave, not give them a hundred reasons to stay.

And this isn't cruel. It's the way of nature. My friends, Brent and Stephanie Wallis (these are not their real names,) understand the concept. They wanted a large family and, by any measure, there home is filled with love and hope and concern for each child. But they also, lovingly concede, the need to stir the nest. It's a hard thing to do – push a child off the edge. But it's the kindest thing we can ever do. We might have to catch one of them periodically to prevent a tragic fall. That's what we call concern. But love, the true love of a parent begins and ends with child chucking. Throw them out, push them off the edge.

It's a brutally hard thing to do. While intentionally making them uncomfortable, jabbing them with sharp sticks, pushing them off cliffs, dumping them off your back, you haven't been cruel, you haven't been unkind, you are not a monster. The fall will terrify them, but they will, eventually, start flapping, they will understand the power of thermals, unseen warm air rising off earth's surface, and as they soar, they will come to recognize that you have endowed them with the greatest gift of all: Flight, and the ability to see the world from new heights that neither you, nor they could have ever imagined.

"I CAN SAY IN ALL HONESTY THAT THE FUTURE DEFINITELY LIES AHEAD."

PAT PAULSEN, COMEDIAN

3
LIVING ON THE EDGE

I retired a few years ago from big city living, and now live in a farming community where I am surrounded by acres and acres of hayfields, grazing cattle, cheese processing plants and ice-cream manufacturing facilities.

We eat enormous amounts of ice-cream here. Farming is big business here. Three commodities lead the way: Alfalfa/Hay, cattle, and dairy products.

Hay is not particularly glamorous, and Utah isn't identified with any unique foodstuff like a lot of other states, probably because humans can't eat hay. You'll recognize many of the various states' "best" consumer products.

Georgia has peaches. California has grapes. Washington has apples. Florida has oranges. Maine has blueberries. Massachusetts has cranberries. Wisconsin has cheese.

I guess our license plates should read, **"Utah, the Cow State."**

Idaho, the land of my birth, is famous for potatoes. Wherever you live in this big old country, you likely see Idaho branded potatoes in your grocery store. Many of the french fries you eat at fast-food restaurants come from Idaho potatoes.

I have first cousins who farm potatoes on thousands and thousands of acres of land, and they have been extremely profitable over the years. My family has spuds on our brain and starch in our DNA. My parents both grew up on Idaho potatoes, so too my grandparents and so did my siblings and I.

Dad knew an imposter potato, and I believe that he could do a blindfold test of different spuds and pick out the true Idahoan every time. The very thought of eating a potato from Maine was anathema to him.

Every fall, Dad made the trek from Salt Lake City up to Burley, Idaho, kind of like salmon swimming upstream and spawning. He would return with an entire pick-up truck full of Idaho potatoes in brown burlap bags and we would feast on them for the next six months. Placed in a cool environment they are remarkably resilient.

And we didn't pay a penny for any of them. We had a pipeline to potato paradise that took care of our potato predilection for many years. Dad would go straight to the fields, armed with a couple of spades, pitchforks, or shovels, and dig them right out of the dirt.

After the fields had been harvested and the crops were all loaded on trucks, making their way to processing plants – and to a McDonald's near you – there were still plenty of potatoes remaining in the corners of the fields, missed by the heavy equipment each time it made a turn. Those corners held hundreds of pounds of nature's gold, and Dad would dig them up, russet roasters, some of which were as large as a football. OK, a small football.

We found riches in the round corners of rectangular fields, and we were content to grab the jewels that everyone else missed. We were comfortable with what we found on the edges, and this concept, in so many ways, helped to shape me and make me comfortable with the broader notion of living on the edge. Taking chances. Exploring new places. Trying new things. And accepting challenges for which I wasn't qualified, meeting new people with fresh ideas and alternative ways to look at life, experiencing, along the way, a variety of successes and failures, both of which taught me new lessons, new strengths, new ideas, and a new degree of toughness and resiliency, like a potato in cold storage, staying fresh all winter. Whether boiled, baked, steamed, shredded, chopped, mashed or french fried, potatoes are always filling and nutritious.

Curiously, we throw away the best part of potatoes – the skin. This is where most of the vitamins are stored, and we toss them. The skins of potatoes provide nearly as much vitamin C and E, as oranges and grapefruit, along with fiber, potassium, and antioxidants. Yet, on Thanksgiving Day, in homes and communities across the country, mountains of good health are hauled to landfills.

Potatoes are a root vegetable and like their cousins, beets, carrots, turnips, rutabagas and parsnips, a potato never sees sunshine until the day it is harvested. We've always been taught that all living plants must have plenty of sunshine to grow, yet potatoes draw their strength from both the green, leafy tops above ground, while simultaneously drawing nutrients straight from the soil. Pity the poor potato. Pity his pathetic appearance. (I wonder what I would look like if I spent my entire life underground.) But with the sun above and the minerals below, gleaning strength from both places, potatoes remind us of all the human qualities we can learn, borrow, and steal from a host of individuals, above us if you will, or below us, all around us, or standing at our side. It's tempting to recall the many times I've had my head underground, or other places where the sun doesn't shine, or make a list of the opportunities I missed, the experiences that passed me by.

It's easy to ignorantly throw out advice and counsel of wise people sitting right in front of us, their wisdom, their insights, frequently adjudged to be garbage, but in the end it's where all the good stuff is.

Perhaps it's time to take a potato pause, munch on some "Gem State" gems, a hot bowl of Idaho's best, and take a moment to consider the corners, living on the edge, rich with rewards for those willing to dig a bit, not afraid of dirty hands, willing to heft one-hundred-pound burlap bags and place them in just the right environment where they are resilient, strong, and survive desperately long, cold winters.

"SOMETIMES WHEN YOU'RE
IN A DARK PLACE YOU THINK
YOU'VE BEEN BURIED.
BUT YOU'VE ACTUALLY
BEEN PLANTED."

CHRISTINE CAINE

MAKE IT A RULE OF LIFE
NEVER TO REGRET AND
NEVER TO LOOK BACK.

REGRET IS AN APPALLING
WASTE OF ENERGY;
YOU CAN'T BUILD ON IT;

IT'S ONLY GOOD
FOR WALLOWING IN.

KATHERINE MANSFIELD.

4

IF I

Two guys are standing in their driveways shooting the breeze about fertilizer, the stock market, and the game last night. A car turns the corner, and a dog runs out, chasing the car, biting the tires. One man says, "That is the stupidest dog." The neighbor says, "No, that's a very smart dog. He believes that one day he'll catch a car, and he never gives up on his dream."

Most dogs have other quirks, oddities, strange behaviors like twirling around a dozen times before settling down on their blanket, or rolling in the smelliest of dead carcasses, that either infuriate us or endear us to them. But they are only doing what their DNA tells them to do. My nine-pound, miniature Schnauzer once treed a bear. True story. He has no idea he is a small dog.

I want to spend a few minutes talking about dogs, specifically their courage, and their innate drive to succeed. I want to talk about dogs who never, never give up. And I want to talk about us, the human species, and what we are chasing.

Recently, out in the parking lot of a shopping center, a car, driven by a remarkably beautiful young woman, passed by me. I gave chase, like an old dog. She saw me coming but didn't show any fear or concern. My cane, my halting gait, and my 70-something shuffle probably had something to do with that.

"I'm sorry to have chased your car through the parking lot. I'm sure it looks creepy."

She shrugged her shoulders.

"Forgive my impertinence," I said, "but I'd like to ask you a question about your license plate."

"Sure," she replied. "Not a problem at all."

"I watched you pull into that parking lot and noticed your plate number. "What does it mean?"

She explained: First, she is from Preston, a small town in Idaho, just across the state line, 20 miles north of me. It is the county seat of Franklin County. In Idaho they have, since 1945, placed on your license plate, the name of the county where you live and where you register your car. Franklin is F, and the numeral "1"differentiates them from Fremont County, number two alphabetically. Her license read, "IF I." This is what caught my eye. To me it read "If I."

She told me it wasn't "IF I", but, rather, a bit of a boast about being the first car registered in Franklin County every year, this honor earned by her grandmother who, for forty years, was the head of the licensing department for the county and was always entitled to the "IF I" plate number. Her grandmother, as

I understand it, retired a few years ago but the family was granted the right, in perpetuity, to that plate.

This young woman indicated that there had been no small amount of bickering and posturing within the family for the right to own the distinct tags, and she was thrilled when grandmother passed them on to her.

She kindly allowed me to take a picture of the plates. "Thank you for your time," I told her. "My questions must sound very odd."

"Not at all," she replied. "That's part of the fun of having the plates. Out of curiosity, why did you stop me?"

"I'm trying to write a book."

"Really, what is it about?" she inquired.

"I guess you could say it's about human behavior, sort of, and the things we are chasing, our dreams, our goals and aspirations, and the success or failure we encounter along the way."

"Very interesting. Thank you for stopping me," she said. "I've never thought of license plates being philosophical. It's been fun to talk with you. Good luck with the book." She then hurried off, back to her errands.

Now here's the thought I had when I spotted the plates. I thought it read "If I." What a great thing to have on your license plates.

"IF I"

These two words have inspired poets and song writers for years. In Rogers and Hammerstein's, Broadway musical "Carousel," Billy sings, "If I loved you."

Gordon Lightfoot (who died on the very day I was writing this) sang, *"If you could read your mind, Love."* Whitney Houston sang, *"If I should stay, I will only be in your way."*

In 1969 at Woodstock, Tim Hardin sang, "If I were a carpenter and you were a lady.

"When poets ask, "If I," it's almost always about unrequited love, or heartbreak. Or regret.

When I saw the Idaho license plate, I began thinking about those two words in a more positive light. The poets have it all wrong. It's not negative, rather the phrase reeks of optimism.

However...

"IF ONLY I"

Now, it is negative, pessimistic when you add just one word, taking on a totally different meaning: "If Only I" This sounds very much like envy. Or jealousy. Or regret. "If only I were like her." If only I had more money." "If only I had spent more time with my kids." "If only I'd gone back to school." If only I had taken that job in Philadelphia. And on and on.

"REGRETS"

Regrets. You've got a million of them in your memory bank, or stored in the cloud, no doubt. Everyone does. Regrets, and its cousins, envy, grudges, bitterness, and resentment are as inborn in us as the quirky habit of dogs chasing cars. We can't help ourselves. We somehow seem to cling to them regardless of how they make us feel, or to what degree they hold us back.

To me, the clever Idaho tag read **"If I"**, the raised letters stamped into metal, giving it an extra sense of permanence, and legitimacy. It sounds like hope, it sounds like strength, it sounds like taking charge of your life, it sounds like courage to do hard things, and the courage to never give up the chase.

If I want success in life, If I want to meet my goals, If I want to conquer my fears, if I want to find joy and contentment, I'm going to have to make it happen myself.

If I want to be a piano player,

PLAY.

If I want to be a singer,

SING.

If I want to be a research scientist,

RESEARCH.

"If I" is synonymous with infinite possibilities. **It is the Doctrine of the Doers. The Mantra of the Movers and Shakers. The Credo of Conquerors.**

Conversely, "If only" feels weighted by waiting, a giant millstone of regret hung round your neck.

If I is about courage and determination.

If Only feels and sounds and smells like fear.

If I is a call to action.

If Only defines all things backward, boring, busted.

And, finally, back to dogs who chase cars and chase bears up trees, undeterred by doubt and fear. **If I** is a manifesto, a universal canine contract, the inviolable standard by which all dogs live. We would be well served if we would adopt, celebrate, and internalize the wisdom of dogs, large or small, from Afghan hounds to Yorkshire terriers, who have universally adopted this formula, who carry no grudges, who know nothing of envy or regrets, who lack any concept of failure, and live the carefree life of confidence, of courage, and of never giving up the chase for the big things that, to some may seem impossible.

> "MY HEART IS FULL OF PAIN,
> AND PERHAPS I'D DESERVE YOU
> AND BE WORTHY OF YOU
> IF I ONLY HAD A BRAIN."
>
> THE SCARECROW, WIZARD OF OZ

5
THE ART OF SELLING

While attending the University of Utah in the nineteen-seventies, I learned any number of things that my classes didn't teach, could never teach. I remember a few things I learned in college, a vague recollection here and there. But the experiences I had in those years, the people I met, are unforgettable.

I think education is about laying down parallel tracks. The first is curriculum, the things that administrators think we need to learn. Professors follow a syllabus without deviation. I call this methodology, rote, recitation, and regurgitation. A professor tells you their view of the facts, the history, the science, all of which you memorize and spit out on a test.

The second track is the stuff that matters, wisdom and understanding, connections to other humans, lessons from the streets, callouses on feet, discovering that strength comes from resistance, balance from walking the razor's edge. I concluded in those years, and the fifty years since, that instead of more textbooks we need more hammers to break molds, blow torches to light more fires.

When I started at the university, I had to park my car in a lot that was about a two-mile walk, up-hill, to the business building complex where a lot of my first semester classes were held.

It's the same lot used for tailgating and parking when there is a big football game, just in front of the stadium on the very far western edge of the campus. Each morning I walked by a curious little building, not really a building, but a small brick structure roughly the size of a single-car garage. I was later told it houses seismic instruments to measure earthquake activity. In my mind it became a symbol of enlightenment and the perfect way to describe the greatest lesson I learned. It is this: Most approaches to teaching young students is to pound into their heads the things others want them to know when we should be encouraging them shake up the world, cause an earthquake, a seismic shift of tectonic plates, challenge everything, and that the smallest structure on campus holds relatively small instruments capable of detecting even the smallest shivers deep in earth's core. Little things teach big lessons.

It was during those same years that I learned one other thing, not a Pythagorean theorem or any other philosophies, puzzles, or postulates; nothing of Plato or Socrates, neither Maimonides, Archimedes, or Thucydides, and nothing enduring from Machiavelli, Mendelev, Nietzsche, Marx, or Kant.

It wasn't anything from a textbook or a lab. It was such a small thing, but It was so profound that it became my personal North Star, my guiding light wherever I went, whatever I was trying to accomplish. I call it "The Italian Tailor Principle." The great philosopher: Aurelio Leone.

Let me tell you about Aurelio.

For a couple of years, I worked in retail, selling men's furnishings, shirts, ties, shoes, socks, belts and all the other things men need to look good. We were paid a crummy hourly wage, but we earned a commission on everything we sold as well. Still, I didn't make a lot of money, but the job provided the flexibility that I needed to go to school and chase girls.

The store was a very high-end men's clothing store, selling expensive, imported suits, classy duds for the upper crust. I worked with a team of other guys who were also going to school, chasing girls, and hovering in the ether just between real adult responsibility and youthful exuberance. Retail always has its slow periods, and we had plenty time to talk and debate the things we were learning and the momentous events of the day which included the war in Viet Nam, Watergate and the crumbling of a presidency, the economy, wage and price controls, and a host of other seemingly important things.

And I learned how to sell. Specifically, I learned how to sell a suit. When we were first hired at the store, we could sell only the items I listed above. There wasn't much commission selling ties and underwear, so we all tried to get the expertise we needed to sell suits. This was where the big commissions were. The manager eventually taught me the finer points of the industry, and I became fluent in the language of thread count, stitches per inch, and all things rakish, snappy and spiffy.

There is an art to selling suits. You might ask how many suits I sold based on thread count. You may be curious to know how many men cared about stitches per inch or the type of wool used. The answer is zero. In the end men don't care about such things.

Here's how to sell a suit:

First, a man walks into the store of his own free-will. He is there for one of two reasons. He's starting a new job or has recently received a big promotion. He is a lawyer, a banker, a businessman and needs to upgrade his wardrobe.

The second type of customer has been dragged in because he has a wedding or a funeral to attend and must have a new suit. The first customer wants a new suit. The second needs a new suit.

For the rest of my career in marketing communications and advertising it was always helpful to differentiate between needs and wants of an audience.

These customers were, for the most part, accompanied by a wife or partner because very few men can be trusted with big, important fashion decisions. The woman, in this case, is your actual customer. Talk to her.

You greet the man or the couple, and after offering a good, firm handshake, they willingly tell me their names, as I determine their taste, somewhere on the conservative/flashy scale. Lawyers, navy blue or black, maybe a pinstripe. Businessmen, a gray glen plaid, or a light, casual tan color.

Next thing, size. Eventually I was able to tell any customer their size with just a quick eyeball scan. Know the customer better than they know themselves. (I closed the largest deal of my career, a seventy-million dollar deal in the high tech industry in San Francisco by conducting dozens of focus groups, at our own expense, and finding details about my clients' market segment that they had never considered. Their image was badly tarnished and didn't know it. We knew more about them than they did.)

Next step, escort them to the suit department, to the racks, and show them the choices in the right size, let's say 42 regular. No talk of thread counts or stitches per inch, just quietly observing their reactions, listening, waiting for the right cue, normally what the female is preferring.

"Let's do this," I suggest. "Let's have him slip on this jacket, make sure it's the right size, see how it looks." If we could get a man to slip on the jacket, we were 25 percent of the way to

a sale. "Not too bad," I comment. "It would need a few alterations but overall, this is a good style for him." Notice my third-
person comments are directed to the woman. She is nodding,
a very good visual cue, and she and I are building rapport.

"Let's take a quick minute and have you slip on the pants,"
I suggest.

"Let me make sure we've got an open dressing room. I am
efficient, courteous, and reassuring. Men need this when making fashion choices."

If we could get a man to try on the pants, in the dressing
room, we seldom lost a sale. Put him in front of a three-way
mirror, let him have a look, then turn to the female and say,
"Doesn't that look good on him?" And she agrees ninety percent of the time because it is new, it is elegant, it is an upgrade
from his old, worn-out suit(s), out of fashion, and a whole lot
better looking than cheap J.C. Penny's alternatives. It does look
good on him. And, it has my approval, important because I'm
jaunty and natty, decked out in the very latest in high-end men's
wear, complete with a silk tie and coordinated pocket square.

I am an expert who can be trusted. These customers are
all older than me, more educated than me, I am trying to be
like them, but for this one moment, in an ironic twist, they want
to be like me. They are now making an emotional decision. No
thread count or other unimportant details. And we don't focus
entirely on how it makes him look, rather on the way that it
makes the two of them feel. We almost never discuss price.
You'll find this hard to believe but it's true. Both buyer and seller
covertly acknowledging that they walked into a high-end shop
by choice, knowing they were going to pay more than any other
store in town.

And now, the closer, Aurelio Leone, the Italian tailor. He has incredible hands, a terrific eye for detail, just enough fussiness to get it exactly right. And the imprimatur of an Italian tailor.

I bring him out from the back room where he works, to the three-way mirror, and ask, "Aurelio, tell me what you think."

He pokes and prods, shakes the shoulders, pinches the waist of the pants, smooths out a few wrinkles in the back, then turns to me and pronounces, "Marco, it's sucha nicea fit." (No offense intended to my Italian friends.)

As this is happening, I am filling out the ticket. We have a 100 percent close rate at this stage. I haven't asked for the sale, or for their approval. I look over the calendar and say to them, "We're looking at about a week to get the final alterations complete. Is that OK, or do you need it sooner?"

"No, a week is just fine," the female offers.

"Great. Aurelio is going to chalk you up. (The measurement marks are made with a piece of tailor's chalk.) And I tell them "Lorraine will have your ticket at the front desk." She is not a cashier, not a clerk, but Lorraine. A human. A personal touch, a family touch. That's the vibe of our place. While that takes place, I escort the wife through the other departments picking out shirts, ties, a silk pocket square, all in colors and patterns that neither of them would have considered on their own.

I ask them if they want to take the shirts and ties now, or if they would prefer that I keep them all together with the suit and have it ready to pick up in a week's time. Again, no haggling on price, no discussions about the ensembles I have recommended. Everything has been based on trust and personal touch. And we just met thirty minutes ago. I didn't just sell them a suit. I sold them a big bag of confidence. I walk them to the front door of the store, shake their hands one more time, wish them well and turn to Aurelio who gives me a smile and a wink.

Next morning, it's back to school where I am hopelessly befuddled by the double helix of DNA strands, part of a required science credit that I would never choose to take, and am spell bound in a psychology class as I learn, for the first time, about Pavlovian responses, these two dichotomous concepts creating a curious contradiction about the essence of who we are, and institutions that attempt to makes us what they want us to be.

If I had to choose, I prefer the education I received while selling suits. Get to know people. Listen carefully. Understand their needs and wants. Cherish personal relationships with others, the deep connections we make with them, and above all, the way they make us feel. *"It's sucha nicea fit."*

I don't remember ever looking back to better understand Crick's double helix but I frequently have drawn on the simple lessons of the humble Italian tailor in the back room, with leathery-tough fingers from a million pin pricks, as he painstakingly, stich-by-stitch by precise stitch, devoted his life to making others feel good while making them look good.

PEOPLE MAY FORGET WHAT YOU SAY, PEOPLE MAY FORGET WHAT YOU DID, BUT THEY WILL NEVER FORGET HOW YOU MADE THEM FEEL.
MAYA ANGELOU

6

ANTIQUE RADIOS

I spent forty years in the ad agency business, crafting campaigns for our clients with clever messaging that our audience would see on television, newspapers, magazines, and a lot of radio. Today you sort of see ads as you are cruising around the internet, and they are targeted right at you.

We would describe our strategy as one-to-many, one ad would reach thousands of people. Today's approach is one-to-one, and advertisers know you so well it starts to feel like they are seeing and hearing everything you say, every purchase you make, your favorite underwear. It's creepy.

I have always been enamored by the radio. Before television, long before streaming cable, radio told us stories, and by "us" I mean my parents' generation. They listened to stories and let their imaginations fill in the cracks. They called it the "theater of the mind." This guided me each time I wrote copy for a client, always looking for a more memorable story.

On one assignment, I hunted down a 1930's era antique radio for some kind of photo shoot we were doing. I found four or five different styles as I poked around the antique stores in town and immediately fell in love with the designs. I thought they were the perfect symbol for an ad agency as we tried to tell stories, in thirty and sixty second bites, that would entertain listeners.

I bought all four of the radios I found. Sometime later I bought another one, then another one, and didn't stop until I had 80 radios in a wide range of styles and colors. I was addicted.

The radios intrigued me for another reason which is what I call "the pity factor." I felt sorry for them, in an odd way, and wanted to take them home and give them a second chance. These treasures had been discarded by someone who no longer wanted or needed the dusty old things. They were seen as trash, and I felt lucky to have found them. My owning them made them valuable again. Shells of early radios, the boxes if you will, that hold the tubes, the wiring, and speakers, were always made of wood. Years later, designers turned to plastic casings, brighter, more colorful, and lighter. And less expensive.

When World War II hit, plastics were in short supply for everything except the war effort, so the radio manufacturers cleverly turned to Bakelite, a hard, smooth-finish material that is made of resins, rather than petroleum used to make plastics. Bakelite was brown, boring and uninspiring, but the designs were revolutionary, dynamic and daring, with round edges and sweeping art deco lines. The shells of the Bakelite radios were nearly as hard as rocks and the workmanship was superior, unlike anything today. The electronic components were solid, so much so that many of the vacuum tubes were enclosed in metal for protection and long life. The first thing visitors to my little radio gallery ask is, "Do they work?" I like grabbing one of them off the shelf and plugging it in to show them. The old tubes take about twenty to thirty seconds to heat up and then the signal comes alive, beginning with a low, dull kind of growl.

My radios have appeared in a variety of ads and movies, borrowed, or rented by locals, and on a couple of occasions by

someone out of state. I've discovered that I'm not the only one who embraces the nostalgia of old things. I have had dozens of people say something like this to me, "Hey, we had an old radio like this when I was a kid. I wonder what happened to it. I'd give it to you if I knew where it was."

I would have gladly taken it.

My father stopped by my office one afternoon, a rare visit, and we talked about radios. He spent his entire career selling them, along with T. V's, and other appliances. He was an expert.

"Where did you get all those radios?" he queried.

"Oh, here and there."

"How long have you been collecting them?"

"Three or four years."

"Why?" he asked. What good are they?"

Some days I ask myself the same question. "It's simple – they're fun to have around – and, they are a great conversation starter. And to me, they're symbols of the changes being made in modern communications and the voices we choose to listen to."

Candidly, neither of these answers made any sense to him.

"Boy, do I remember radios like this," he said. "I've seen more radios than you can possibly imagine. I suppose you could blame me for their decline."

This was something I'd never heard before. He had my undivided attention.

The very short version of his story is that he worked on both the retail and the wholesale sides of the appliance industry, once being recruited to manage the appliance department of a department store.

"I used to sell radios like these," he began. "But when stereo technology came along everyone wanted the fancy new, HiFi's, not radios. When our wholesaler came by, I asked about pricing. My reaction was that they were a little steep for most families. I wanted a quantity discount.

"I told him the price I'd be willing to pay, and he just laughed. He said that in order to get that price I'd have to buy an entire train load of the things." Dad paused, grinning.

"You bought an entire train load, didn't you," I prodded.

"Two," he replied. "I eventually bought two train loads because the fool gave me such a good price. I knew everyone in town would buy the new stereos once they heard about them. Especially at the price I would be able to offer."

"Did you sell them all?"

"Not right at first. I had to promote them a bit so I ran an ad in the newspaper telling people to bring in their old radios, in any condition, and I would give them fifty bucks toward a new stereo. It enabled families to get rid of their old radios and get the new technology at a price that they couldn't afford to pass up.

"The old radios stared pouring in the door. Dozens of them each day and I didn't know what to do with them, so I cleared out one of the front display windows along the main street and we started throwing them in there. As the pile started getting bigger, it created more interest, more demand for the stereos."

"Throwing them in?" I said. "You just threw them in? Like throwing out the trash?

"Yep. Big pile. Hundreds and hundreds of them, just like some of these here in your collection. I wish I had a few of them. I'd give them to you," he said with a smile.

"Yeah, yeah, yeah, I've heard that before. What eventually became of them?" I winced.

"Well, as I recall, we backed up a big truck and loaded the radios in it. Then we hauled them to the dump out south of town. Might have been two truckloads. Yes, probably two trucks. There were a lot of radios."

The dump! (Excuse me, I mean the sanitary landfill.) He took several thousand old radios to the dump. "Didn't you realize that they would be valuable one day?" I asked. "Didn't you realize how beautiful they were? How could you just throw them away?"

His wise answer: "How could I have possibly known? How do you know today what will be valuable tomorrow? What was I supposed to do with all those radios while we waited fifty years for people to discover that yesterday's junk is today's treasure?"

There was a time when radio broadcasts were like today's Google search engine, the source of news and information. President Franklin Roosevelt talked to a nation about war, comforted by just hearing his voice.

The story is told of a lonely shepherd who spent long days and nights with only his dog and his violin. And his radio. He wrote a letter to Arturo Toscanini, the famed conductor of the NBC orchestra in the thirties and forties, asking him for a favor.

One evening Toscanini stepped to the microphone and told his audience this: "Before we begin our program, I've been asked to sound a long, loud middle C so that a shepard in the faraway hills can tune his violin." The airways hushed for one minute, nothing but a long, loud middle C played by the hands of a master cellist.

I regularly go antique hunting, from store to store, city to city, finding unique trinkets and baubles that have very little value except to the person holding it. I delight in artifacts from attics, trash that becomes treasures, gifts of gold, presents from the past. Throwaways transformed by time into trophies.

The musings in this book have focused on the journeys we take; the roads we travel; each milestone we reach; the footsteps we follow; the clashes and the compromises; our critics and our comrades; moving forward with certainty or the complete lack of it; the things that get us moving or the things that freeze us in our tracks, the common denominator generally being fear; confidence or cowardice; the givings and the takings; the compromises and the complaints; the advice we either heed or ignore; the voices we choose to listen to, internal voices that say "I want to," and the contradictory external voices that say "you never will;" the hands we have held, pats on the back and kicks in the rear, and the occasional loss of a guiding signal.

Like the radios in my gallery that people got tired of, we often get rid of things in favor of sleeker, shiner newer models. We regularly discard philosophies, teachings, ideas, people, and especially values that some think are useless and worn out, unable to see potential and promise. It's easy to get distracted by the things we don't have, or the large pile of regrets we have stacked up, causing us to miss a mile marker and lose our way.

Just knowing that there are several thousand gems buried under fifty years of garbage in a local landfill, adds value to the few radios I have. Still, there is something unnerving, haunting, about knowing all those treasures are under there somewhere, non-biodegradable, brown Bakelite. I periodically wake up from a dream where I see a golden light deep in the ground, the glow of a thousand radio tubes warming up, ready for a second chance, ready to broadcast a long loud middle C to get us back in tune, back on the road, moving, once again... to the next milestones that lie just ahead.

"THERE ARE FAR BETTER THINGS AHEAD THAN ANY WE LEFT BEHIND."
C.S. LEWIS

7
LESSONS FROM A CARPENTER

There is a desk, a dresser, a couple of stools and one, maybe two bookcases still around that my grandfather made. They're made of inexpensive grades of wood and are either painted or treated with a very dark stain which hide the flaws of the wood. Even though they qualify as antiques by virtue of their age, they wouldn't be worth anything if you tried to sell them. That doesn't much matter because no one would dream of selling them. After all, Grandpa crafted them by hand, without a blueprint or diagram of any kind. He simply made them up as he went along. He never received training yet was a master of the craft. As it turns out, his furniture is more practical than pretty, and while his pieces are short on aesthetics, they are very long on sentiment.

I once met a man who thought he knew my grandfather and asked if he had been an attorney. I explained that Grandpa didn't have a formal education and that he was just a humble carpenter. That man was quick to remind me of another great man who was a just a humble carpenter.

On one of our annual summer camping trips, we strayed off the beaten path and set up camp alongside a river in a remote, heavily forested area somewhere in Wyoming, far, far away from the heavily regulated, crowded campgrounds in Jackson Hole, or Yellowstone. Too many tourists. Too much civilization. Too many rules and restrictions.

First afternoon, after unpacking the car and helping Dad pitch the tent, Grandpa grabbed my shoulder and said, "Come with me." This is at the top of my list of favorite experiences, just Grandpa and I walking into the evergreen forest. He took his time finding just the right trees, straight and uniform in diameter. We took only dead trees, still standing upright but killed by harsh winters. They were perfectly aged. I took a turn with the axe under the tutelage of a real-life lumberjack as we cut them to a uniform length. We used a hatchet to remove all the brittle branches.

We stacked them neatly together, four in all, and hoisted them onto our shoulders. Back in camp, armed with just his hatchet, no saw, no measuring tape, no nails or screws, Grandpa built, a picnic table. For roughly a dozen days this is where we ate our meals, played card games, read comic books, and whittled sticks. The table built by grandpa and me. My jealous brothers reminded me that the only thing I really did was haul the logs into camp. But I still boasted about it.

I learned a lot of great things from Grandpa, although carpentry wasn't one of them. When there is remodeling or fix-it work to be done, I head straight to Anji's List or some other internet tool. Sure, I have a few manly tools and I know which end of the hammer to use, but it might just as well be a saxophone for all the skill it would take for me to use either one.

In the process of sawing, hammering, leveling and measuring, it is incredibly beneficial to have a good eye and a firm hand. My grandfather had a very good eye. Even in his seventies he continued to do occasional jobs for people, such as, adding on a room, remodeling a kitchen. Good carpenters are like well-made tools – they just won't quit.

But eventually tremors in Grandpa's hands forced him to. You may be able to cheat a little on measuring a board – that's what planes and sandpaper are for. And you can always get a straight line with the help of a plumb bob or a level – besides, if something is just a hair crooked, the human eye can't catch it anyway. But a hand that shakes and trembles has no business pushing boards through a nine-inch cross-cut blade on a table saw. Power tools are somehow like horses and dogs. They can sense fear, uncertainty, tentativeness.

And shaky hands.

Also, power tools can kick like a horse and bite like a dog if you turn your back or fail to pay attention for just a moment. Ripping a board requires a steady hand and my grandfather had lost his. The saw sensed it.

One day Grandpa called my dad to say he had cut his hand, insisting that he would be fine. Dad didn't believe him. Grandpa already had one of those stubby fingers that most carpenters have. He was used to a cut every now and then and didn't like complaining. As Dad pressed him for more details, he admitted that he might lose one or two of his fingers, but at his age he wasn't going to worry about it. In other words, he had nearly cut off his hand. Thanksgiving was coming, so it wasn't a problem to make the trek to Idaho a few days earlier than planned.

A local doctor gave him a tetanus shot to prevent infection, sewed him up, dressed the massive wound and sent him home. What else could he do? It seemed like the doctor knew what he was doing, so we all enjoyed Thanksgiving dinner and a few days of the farm life we all loved.

Two days later, Grandpa was dead. An allergic reaction to his tetanus shot set in, beginning with numbness to his feet and eventually creeping up through his lower extremities and paralyzing his vital organs. At the small, local hospital, every effort was made to save him, but nothing worked. An ambulance drove him all the way to Salt Lake City and a much larger, more advanced hospital. The doctors concluded that it was Guillain-Barre syndrome, brought on by a severe, extremely rare reaction to the tetanus shot. In the sixties there were no standardized potency guidelines for tetanus and Grandpa was administered the wrong dose. There would be talk of a malpractice suit, but my elders quickly rejected the idea.

This was my first experience with death, and it was not a good one. I had a hard time coping with the irony that one of his own tools killed him.

Grandpa was old. He was wobbly when he walked, had afternoon naps, and wore dentures. And then there were those tremors in his hands. He was 72 when he died. As I write this, I am 72 and have shaky hands. Age is such a relative thing.

It wasn't until years later that I saw the big picture and concluded that as each of us, all of us, stumble and bumble, fall, falter and fail, count the opportunities we missed, the messes we made, the goofs, the gaffes, the foibles, the stubbornness, the arrogance, the fish that got away, the girl that got away, people you drove away, the bad judgements you made, the broken fences you didn't bother to mend, that it isn't always the cut that kills, but the medication that is prescribed. A botched diagnosis leads to a botched treatment, the wrong medicine, or our refusal to take the medicine.

We frequently chose to stay broken. I'm still learning that concept and watch with incredulity as people I know experience severe, self-inflicted wounds brought on by bad choices, bad decisions, who walk dangerously close to the edge of cliffs, play with fire, juggle chain saws, and haven't learned that those with shaky hands should never mess with sharp objects. Many are inflicting serious wounds and assume that they can patch everything up with a band-aid when they really need a tourniquet. Paralysis of the heart and mind is highly likely for those of us who fail to cleanse a wound, or simply seek temporary measures to mask the pain.

My grandfather's handmade furniture might not look like much to you. But. for me, it's a constant reminder that there is still much I can learn from a humble carpenter gone these many years.

"I MAY NOT HAVE GONE
WHERE I INTENDED TO GO,
BUT I THINK I HAVE ENDED UP
WHERE I NEEDED TO BE."

DOUGLAS ADAMS

8
SELFIES AND SELFISH

There's a new baby at our house. Well, not quite at our house, but in our family. I almost forgot how grandmothers go crazy for new babies, snatching them from their mothers, swaddling and cuddling them, speaking the universal goo-goo-ga-ga language of mothers and grandmothers everywhere, chewing endlessly on their fat cheeks. Mothers care for their babies. Grandmothers eat them.

Good news: We have a new baby. The very, very bad news is that he made my daughter a grandmother, and me, a great grandfather. I'm still uncomfortable with my new title.

I met my great-grandfather, Mitchell, a couple of times, a frail 95 year-old with a long, white beard permanently stained with a yellow and brown streak running down the middle of it, fifty years of chewing tobacco and spitting it at random chickens strolling by.

Great-grandfathers are always old, musty, nearly deaf, right? Well, I am none of the above, but someday this little boy will see my liver spots and smell my mustiness. Until then, he's a tasty snack each time I see him.

When the first-born child comes along in a family we take pictures by the thousands, cataloging everything he does, as if he is the last child on earth. We frequently must add more storage to our phones to accommodate all the photos and there is

53

real danger that even the mighty cloud will explode.

I tell people that I was never a baby. Nor was I ever a child, or a little schoolboy. There is no evidence of any of this, not a single photograph in any scrapbook. It's as if I spontaneously appeared on the planet, surprising everyone in my family. "Oh look, there is a sixteen-year-old boy living with us. Where did he come from?"

I am the fourth child in a large family, and I've concluded that, apparently, I wasn't worthy of the cost of taking a picture of me. I did find an old black-and-white shot of my brother and me holding up a very long stringer of trout, the focus of the shot being the fish. Oh, look, here's me in cap and gown on graduation night, one single, fuzzy photo taken with a camera from a bygone era.

That's about it. No photos anywhere. My story should be titled, "The boy who fell from the sky."

But there is another story about all the pictures we now take. At many of our family gatherings, we keep phones/cameras at the ready, always on, snapping shots of the kids, or taking selfies of us with the kids, or of siblings, or of the plate of food we just loaded up. At the end of the evening, I have amassed roughly a hundred new photos, and most of the other family members have at least this many or more. Before we load everyone into SUV's, minivans and pickup trucks and head home, we huddle around in a circle and airdrop every photo we have onto everyone else's phone.

In total for just that evening, I have nine hundred new photos to review, (I'm rounding up) and a plan to delete duplicates and the shots where someone has their eyes closed. But I never do. They are all such good photos, shot with my new I-phone 14 Pro with a camera that is on par with professional cameras.

Of the nine hundred photos taken this evening, I eventually delete a paltry dozen or so.

We've all gone mad for photography, every pocket on every pair of denim jeans bulging with a 2"x5" rectangle, the new version of a gun in a holster worn by cowboys in the wild, wild, west, ready to draw and shoot anyone who suggests a duel at the OK Corral.

I recall the day when a salesman came to my office trying to sell me one of the very first mobile, cellular phones. These early devices were roughly the size of our old '53 Buick, and their semi-official name was "the brick." They didn't hold much of a charge, and coverage was limited. I recall telling the salesman, "I sit here, in my office most of every day. Why do I need a mobile phone?" He reassured me that everyone will eventually have such a device and I finally agreed to buy two of them, one for me, one for my biz dev guy. To close the deal, the phone salesman finally tossed in a free wheelbarrow to carry them around in.

I was slow, at first, to adopt some of the new tech devices, but when I found out how convenient the mobile phone was, how it increased productivity, I became a convert, seeing the vision of a tech future, and embracing desk-top publishing, networking everyone in our office, eventually growing our ad agency around business-to-business tech clients. We became a very prominent agency, buying more ad space in the early days of Apple computers than any other marketing firm, and for two or three years we were invited to sit at the head table of award shows hosted by two leading tech publications.

I went all in on tech.

Now, looking out my window through the lens of a retired, old, great-grandfather and washed up ad guy, my version of spitting tobacco at a chicken is to bitch and moan about technology. The new innovations blessed my life and helped make me successful businessman. I am in the camp of those who wonder, "How did we live without them?"

But I have now come to see the dangers as well, not as a crabby old man, but as a respected early member of the technology revolution. I don't want to engage in a food fight, or a battle of words or intentionally denigrate anyone or any institution about their use of these tools. And I certainly don't want to be seen as a hypocrite who simultaneously lives and breathes technology while at the same time condemning it.

But when I see so many people, both young and old, staring into their phones for 3-4 hours at a time, I see children who are not outside throwing a football, or riding a bike, or interacting with others of the human species. I see an entire generation of men bonding with machines instead of bonding with women, the easy access to violent games and pornography sucking the life out of them. Tens of millions of people around the globe prefer communicating with strangers scattered here and there, rather than those who are standing right next to them. I hear the voices of the "look at me" generation who, in staggering numbers, are developing mental health problems that swirl and tangle the brain with the poison of perceived perfection and the "I'll never be as good" pandemic.

A few years ago, we stood at Trevi Fountain in Rome, and then climbed the Spanish Steps, unable to count all the tourists taking selfies of themselves at these ancient architectural marvels, capturing the perfect image of themselves for their social media posts. These selfies seemed more important than the historical sites themselves. Cellular phones, along with the cameras built into them and the dozens of apps we load on them, transform them into powerful computers enabling us to conduct business from anywhere, join important online meetings, attach documents to a text message, and download enormous digital artwork files just in time for tomorrow's board meeting. Businessmen and women love this.

On a very personal note, I now have serious health issues I'm dealing with, but I can manage every aspect of my care, monitor my heart rate, count the steps I walk, keep track of my meds and remind me when to take them and stay connected with my doctors. I am a fanatic about technology and the powerful, magical solutions they provide for me.

Still, it all worries me. I will take neither the soap box, the podium, nor the pulpit to condemn, rather, to caution. You will have to decide for yourself and your family, the good and the bad, the possibilities and the precautions, the tools that will build tomorrows or the dynamite that destroys them.

Here's one way of looking at it.

Phone. Photo. Phony.

Take a quick look at these three words. At a glance they look almost identical. Change one or two letters and, while different, they are inextricably linked. (I have been collecting words like this for many years, referencing many of them in my writings. Check out the title of this book, **Millstones and Milestones**.)

The technology of the digital age is all about social connections, a very good thing. But with no boundaries, no fences, the staggering number of photos we take of ourselves has created a digital pandemic that is phony, phake, and phictitous. I believe we are at the end of the digital era, and we are now well into, what history will describe as the "Selfish Epoch."

My thoughts about all of this finally synthesized when a news feed from **CNN** popped up on my **Google** browser with this headline:

"Indian official drains reservoir
to retrieve phone dropped while taking selfie."

The author of the article, Kunal Sehgal, reports this: *"A government official in India who drained a reservoir to retrieve a phone he dropped while taking a selfie has been suspended from his job. More than 528,000 gallons of water were pumped out of the Paralkot reservoir, over a period of four days, in an effort to retrieve the Samsung handset belonging to Rajesh Vishwas, a local food inspector.*

"Vishwas had been out with friends last Sunday afternoon when it slipped from his grasp at the scenic spot in the central Indian state of Chattisgarh."

His version of events is at odds with that of his employer, who suspended him on the grounds of misusing his position — noting he had wasted hundreds of thousands of gallons of water at a time of severe heat.

His suspension order, seen by **CNN**, also claims that Vishwas did not receive permission to drain the water."I read this article and thought, *"Those must be really important selfies."* While this is an extreme incident, it helps bring into focus the value we place on our face, and the fact that we are taking increasing numbers of photos of ourselves, showcasing only the very best of us so others don't see the rest of us, more and more of us joining the look-at-me brigade, camouflaging what has become a world where selfies make us more selfish and our minds are filled with **Phiction, Phakery, Phraud, and Phoniness.** I'm going to continue to embrace new technology, I am going to continue taking pictures, but I'm sure as hell not going to drain an entire reservoir just to save a few self-indulgent photos. Each of us, all of us, are thriving and growing, exponentially expanding our minds, the bright lights of technology guiding us down the road of endless possibilities. Personally, I can't wait to see what's ahead, hoping that artificial intelligence doesn't eventually take over our brains. To a certain extent, with piles and piles and piles of selfies as evidence, it seems, to a certain extent, that it already has.

"SOME PEOPLE ARE REAL. SOME PEOPLE ARE GOOD. SOME PEOPLE ARE FAKE. AND SOME PEOPLE ARE REAL GOOD AT BEING FAKE."

AUTHOR UNKNOWN

9
FREE EGGS

I've discovered a few of things about raising chickens. I've only been at it for five or six years, so I'm not an expert. Here are a few observations.

Pecking Order.

You've heard this term. You've probably used this term. It's a real thing. You can't mix old with young because the jealous older hens will peck the younger girls to death. It happens inside chicken coops just like in offices, businesses, a prison cell block.

Mating.

Lots of people ask how that happens. Your very first guess is the right one. A rooster is needed of course, and don't worry, you do not consume fertilized eggs because a layer hen lives out her entire life keeping her vows of celibacy, a novitiate in a convent.

Cost of Eggs.

At the suggestion of friends, I selected chickens that lay only brown eggs, known to have more nutrients and a much darker yolk. People tell us how lucky we are to have free, fresh eggs every day. With a quick calculation I estimate that just one of our "free eggs" costs us around two dollars.

This may be a slight exaggeration, but chicken feed, called "Layer Pellets" is about $65 for a 25-pound sack. We buy four bags each time we go **Intermountain Farmers** and walk out with a receipt for $260.

Add to that the cost of equipment: I built a coop and fencing, bought drip-water feeders, one that hangs under the nest, another larger one on the ground outside. In the winter I have to run power from the house out to the coop so I can plug in the warming base that prevents water from freezing in the winter.

While at the farm store, I grab a bag of scratch, made up of grains, seeds, and a whole bunch of dehydrated worms. This gives the birds additional nutrients. More worms, bigger eggs. I buy two large bags, sprinkle some around the chicken pen and watch the girls go crazy.

Oh, wait, I forgot the diatomaceous earth, some kind of white powder that you add to the regular pellets for a stronger shell. Roughly $50 bucks a bag.

Don't go back and add all this up. I didn't. I don't really care. It's been fun to have the hens around. The amount of guano they leave behind is staggering, fantastic fertilizer for my flowers when mixed with some dirt and compost to cool it down. I gladly buy all this stuff, happily trudging out to the coop each day to collect four or five eggs.

That's not very many, but it is two-dozen each week.

Two dozen eggs for free.

One other important lesson I've learned: Chickens die. I've never slaughtered one of the birds for meat, it's just not something I could ever do. They become pets and squat down at my feet, a signal that they want to be cuddled. Margo will let you hold her and pet her the way you would a dog. (Yes, they all have names.)

Over the course of the last six years, I have dug graves and buried a dozen and a half birds. Three of them from some sort of malady, all the others killed by predators, like foxes, racoons, and dogs. One morning, six of them were slaughtered by the otherwise, sweet cockapoo next door. Our daughter's dog. No further comment.

I took extra precautions but still, the murders continued. I wasn't just protecting my eggs. Nor was I simply protecting birds, I was protecting Margo, she had a name, my favorite girl with the beautiful gray and white markings identifying her as a member of the Barred Rock family.

I routinely walked out to the coop one evening to make sure they were all bedded down for the night. (Quick note, I built four nests for them, layer boxes, and lined them with wood shavings, and assumed they would sleep in these cozy beds. They don't. They sleep all night on a stick, clinging to it with their feet. Give that a try sometime.)

It's dark up here in farm country, very dark, so I grabbed a flashlight to make my nightly rounds. There was something wrong inside. There was an eerie feeling. The girls were quiet but nervous, uneasy. Margo looked me in the eye and jerked her head to the left, the type of nod humans sometimes use to point out someone or something without using our fingers. I opened my eyes wide as if to say to Margo, "What?" She nodded again, this time more pronounced. I understood. Something else was in the coop. I nodded my understanding, and slowly panned the room with my flashlight.

Eastern wall, down in the corner, crouched in a ball, the enemy you hope you never have to meet: Skunk.

"Don't panic, don't panic," I told myself. Margo gave me a covert scowl, as if to say, "Do something. You can't just stand there. What's the matter, are you chicken?"

Slowly, silently I backed out, my feet as heavy as two cement blocks. Outside the protective fence, I stood completely still, reached into my pocket for my cell phone. Margo desperately whispers, "You can't kill a skunk with a cell phone. Get a gun." Well, I'm not a gun owner. Go to option B, Get a bull horn and tell the smelly varmint to come out with his hands up? Probably not.

Option C, "Hey Siri, call Jud Eades." My son-in-law next door answers the phone, and I do that sort of screaming whisper, adding urgency to my voice, fully aware I could frighten the skunk.

"What's wrong?" he asks.

"Skunk. Coop. Gun."

Puzzled, he says, with a little laugh, "What?"

I'm now chilly, shivering, afraid to move, keeping eyes on the predator. He's looking back at me, his fear running about as high as mine. I could have shut the door and made a run for the house but that would have left a skunk alone with the brood of hens, eight of them with names and personalities. I argued with myself, rationalizing, "These two-dollar eggs we get aren't worth all of this. I'm out of here."

Jud is still on the phone. "What's going on?"

"I have a 211 in progress. I have eyes on the perp. Be advised, he is armed and dangerous. I need backup. Bring....."

Before I finish saying, "Bring a gun," Jud is standing next to me.

"Will this do?"

Turns out it is a modified assault rifle, specifically a .556 military grade assault rifle.

"That should do the job," I comment, knowing absolutely nothing about guns."There's a skunk in the chicken coop."

"Awesome." He is thrilled to take charge.

The gun has been pre-loaded, he's ready to go. He raises the rifle to his shoulder, takes careful aim. I notice his shaking hands. He is as scared as me. He later denied it.

"POP." A single shot.

"Did I get him?"

"I don't know. You had a high-powered rifle pointed at him,

you tell me," I insisted.

"You've been shining the light in there the whole time," he barks back. "Didn't you see anything? What happened?"

Pause. Big swallow. "He's married to my daughter," I thought. "Be nice." Pause. "I think you missed."

Jud owns about 30 guns, maybe more, locked in a safe. He loves to hunt, but mostly he likes to collect them. I've never gone hunting with him, but we have taken the boys out to the gun range so he can teach them the right way to handle a weapon. We shoot clay pigeons, targets, soft-drink cans. He's an expert marksman.

"What happened?" he repeats, anxiously.

"I think you missed," I say again, a bit more firmly.

"We can't be more than ten yards away," he snaps incredulously. "I had him right in the crosshairs of my scope. I never miss. I did not miss him. Now go in there and see if he's alive or wounded."

"OH, OK boss. No problem. I'll just saunter on over and check to see if there is possibly a wounded skunk. Happy to check it out." He picks up the sarcasm.

"I'm not going in there," I insist.

He tells me in no uncertain terms, "They're your chickens, it's your coop, it's your problem and I'm not about to go in there."

I reply, "If you hadn't missed a point-blank shot, one of the most important shots you'll ever take, we wouldn't be dealing with any this."

We weren't fighting, we like each other very much. It was frustration coupled with fear that got our cortisol and our testosterone boiling over. Take a breath. Calm down. Go check it out.

Together, we go inside the coop. First quick glance, nothing. There aren't many places to hide in a chicken coop. In fact, there's nowhere to hide in a small chicken coop. Nothing. This was one magical skunk who dodged a bullet and vanished into thin air.

Next morning, terrified that the beast may have come back during the night and wiped out the source of my free eggs, I return to the scene of the crime. It's July, it's hot, and I don a ski parka, ski hat, ski gloves and googles, a makeshift protective outfit, dreading the spray of an angry skunk.

No sign of his return or his whereabouts. It was a skunk, I am certain. There was no mistaking it. A very bushy black ball with a white stripe down its back. I knew what a skunk looked like from watching Pepe LePew, one of the stars of Warner Brothers' cartoons. Judson agreed we didn't have hallucinations or wild imaginings. It was a skunk.

And Judson admitted he badly missed the shot. He had previously set the parameters for the scope on high-power but didn't account for such a close-up shot. He should have aimed higher. It was a scientific anomaly, not human error. Internal affairs cleared us both of incompetence.

The skunk didn't magically vanish that night. The light of day revealed loose dirt and a very small hole under the dirt floor of the coop. The hole was not much bigger than, say a lemon, maybe a bit smaller, but this poultry predator, the size of a large cat, crawled in through that very small hole he had made, and exited back through it when he heard gunfire, stealthily crawling back into the night.

For the next two days I tilled up the soil around the coop and laid down some wire fencing, flat on the ground, coved it up onto the walls, kind of like coved floor covering in your house, covered it all with soil, and put large boulders around it so skunks couldn't burrow under the dirt floor. I had become a designer of security systems for predator protection. A trip to Home Depot for all the right fencing set me back around $200, adding additional costs to my "free eggs."

I no longer raise chickens or collect fresh eggs. Not because of the curious case of the vanishing skunk in the nighttime, nor because of the rising cost of maintaining chickens. Scary black beasts of the barnyard don't haunt my dreams. It was a fun hobby. I've moved on. The red farmyard-style coop keeps a lonely watch over the barren barnyard. I'm keeping it just in case Margo one day wanders back in. And I'm keeping my eyes alert for disruptions in the dark, those of my own making and those of strangers, predators, thieves, blaggards, and midnight marauders outside my door, intent on stealing from me my best intentions, my hopes, my unmet goals.

One day you may be baffled and befuddled by predators. For all your efforts at prevention, they will continue to skulk around, preying in the darkness, cowards that they are, hiding in the shadows, vanishing in the light of day leaving you to wonder, "Where did they go?" and, "Where did I go wrong?"

When someone you admire, standing right at your side, looks over and says to you, "You missed the shot," chances are pretty good you missed the shot. Terror, testosterone, and fear of failure will often cause that to happen. You are, from time to time, going to miss a shot, but you're stronger because of your willingness to take the shot.

Predators are coming for you in a variety of villainous ways, a lengthy list that includes plagues, disease, unrequited love, enemies who call you friend, friends that will stick a switch blade between your ribs, jealous co-workers, unreasonable employers, inflation, sky-rocketing prices that have your family swimming in debt, setbacks and disappointments that have you drowning in doubt, bad marriages, bad advice and bad decisions. They are all skunks. And they stink. They are cunning, they are vile, these nocturnal nuisances, and they won't quit. You can put up miles and miles of fencing and rock walls to keep them out, still they lurk.

But you can go on, confidently, fearlessly, because you know they are out there, and after a few frightening encounters, you're ready to confront them head on. And beat them. You're not afraid because you have tussled with trouble before. You may have to recalibrate your scope, you may have to recalibrate your aim, but regardless of your fears, your trembling hands, take a breath, move carefully, and remember that there is no such thing as boogey men, and by the way...

...there is no such thing as free eggs.

THINK POSITIVE.
FOR EXAMPLE: I FELL DOWN
THE STAIRS TODAY AND THOUGHT,
"WOW, I SURE FELL DOWN
THOSE STAIRS FAST."

AUTHOR UNKNOWN

10
SQUEEZING CIDER

"You're a salesman aren't you?"

I turned to see if the old fellow was talking to me. He was. "No," I replied. "I work in advertising. I'm not a salesman." I thought my large black leather portfolio and briefcase made me look like an architect. It was the look I was going for. He only saw a salesman.

"Advertising. Sales. Same thing. I'm pretty good at figuring people out, you know. You're a salesman, alright."

I introduced myself to him.

"My names Henry," he returned. "I'm glad to meet you. I've been stuck here at the airport for nearly two hours. I guess I missed my bus."

We were at the Seattle airport, and I was also waiting for the shuttle bus to my hotel. I had a big presentation the next morning. I didn't mind sharing a few minutes with Henry, an eighty-four-year-old man from Nevada. As it turned out, it was a long few minutes. And some of the most enjoyable I can remember at a crowded airport.

"I missed my bus by about five minutes," Henry continued. I got mixed up and missed it. I get mixed up a lot these days. But the bus to Mercer Island will come if I keep waiting."

I checked the schedule for him and told him that he had about another 15 minutes to wait.

"I knew it. I knew it would come. Usually does if you keep waiting."

"What's on Mercer Island?" I inquired. "Why are you going there?"

"The apple harvest. I've been coming now for over 40 years with my friends. We make apple cider. It's harder now, turning the ornery crank of the apple press. You know that I'm eighty-four?"

"Yes, you mentioned that you're eighty-four. Several times already."

"Well, making cider isn't as easy as it used to be. I can tell you that," Henry chastised.

I asked him how he got to be eighty-four, and I meant it. I really did want to know how someone gets to be that old and stays so happy. Sure, Henry was a little confused, and he missed a lot of buses, but he looked very happy, very robust.

"That's a good question," he said. "I don't smoke or drink. I had most of my stomach removed in '47 and in '80 I had a synthetic aorta put in. In '87 I had a triple bypass. I've never been on a golf course. I've never picked up a bowling ball or a tennis racket. Fact is I haven't done much of anything. I'll be gad danged if I know why I'm still alive. It just seems that things have gone my way." (He didn't cuss but said it just this way.)

I reminded him that he had squeezed a lot of apple cider over the years and speculated on whether 40 years of drinking the stuff had anything to do with his longevity. "You know, 'an apple a day keeps the doctor away' theory." I wondered if this may be the secret of life for my eighty-four-year-old friend, Henry.

He pulled up short and said, "Well, I guess so. Sure, can't hurt. I just happen to like cider."

The conversation moved to politics. Henry said that he generally voted Republican even though he had been advised not to. "My grandfather would never tell you if he was a Republican or a Democrat. He always said, 'Never vote for the party. Vote for the man.' And I can tell you, my grandfather always stuck with that philosophy. He always voted for the man – just as long as that man was a Republican."

We both had a good laugh. Henry had this joke well-rehearsed, and I knew he had told it many times before. No matter, he laughed as hard as I did.

Our buses came at the same time, and I found myself wishing we had another 15 minutes to spend together. I'm not sure I would have wanted a whole week of Henry's bad jokes, but waiting at a bus stop one afternoon was delightful.

I shook Henry's hand, and he said, "Good luck, kid." To octogenarians, everyone is a kid.

"Good luck to you, too, Henry. And thanks for keeping me company," I added. "I've enjoyed talking with you." I was happy to know he had gotten on the right bus.

Henry taught me a few life lessons that day. I call them **"Henry's Rules for Living."** They go something like this:

1. **We all get mixed up occasionally, but usually the bus will come again.**
2. **Things have a way of working out in the way that is right for you. There are times in our lives when this doesn't seem possible, but Henry has it just about right.**
3. **Drink lots of apple cider. It may not give you a longer life, but it sure can't hurt.**
4. **Always vote for the man, as long as that man is a Republican.**

5. Stop and talk with interesting people at airport bus stops. Or planes, or trains. Wherever your travels take you, you never know what you might learn. Go home, write down whom you met and how they made you feel. I guarantee you'll learn some interesting things.

I salute Henry and his adventure to Mercer Island. I do love a good glass of cold cider in the fall. My neighbors have an annual cider-pressing day, similar to what Henry described to me.

I would guess that approximately 30 people come each year to celebrate the harvest and raise a glass to friends. There is an entrance fee to the event: Apples. Don't show up without some to add to the mix. Don't worry about what variety you have; any apple will do. Make sure you bring sharp knives and any bottle, empty milk carton, any container you have around. You're going to need plenty of containers.

On the appointed Saturday, cars and trucks and trailers arrive, and within thirty minutes there are bushel baskets, cardboard boxes, and any number of orange, five-gallon plastic buckets emblazoned with the **Home Depot** logo. Apples, apples everywhere, but not a drop of cider to drink. Not yet.

It looks like organized chaos. There are no assignments made, no foreman cracking the whip, everyone has been coming for years and they know what to do. A dozen or so folks are sitting at long picnic tables, sharp knives in hand, cutting the fruit, basically, into four pieces, and filling up buckets, the core, the seeds, the skins included.

There is a line of team members, kind of like an old fire brigade, passing buckets from person to person, from the cutting tables to the antique wooden press where the colorful kaleidoscope of apples await their turn into the hopper. Down they go.

I don't like sitting all afternoon chopping apples so you can generally find me with a wooden paddle in hand, nudging the fruit down the chute. Then I take a turn at the hand crank, turning the gears, squeezing out the elixir of the gods. Even the strongest of the men last for just twenty minutes at the crank, a big, heavy piece of human-powered steel.

The pressing halts for a minute or two while the mesh filter is cleaned, sometimes replaced. This is where seeds and skin all end up, only the juice making it into the final product. The resulting mash is taken in heavy buckets and dumped over the fence where it becomes feed for the sheep.

Then, here comes the prize, liquid gold, streaming out of the machine, gallon after gallon, moved by another fire brigade with the tenderness of passing a baby, careful not to spill a single drop.

Bring your containers to the filling station, put a funnel at the top, and fill 'em up.

My mouth is watering just writing about it. I fill myself a plastic cup, and hold it up to the autumn sun where it takes on a glow of pure, earthy goodness.

It isn't apple juice, that cheap imposter you get at the store. This is cider so it is cloudy, textured, full-bodied, rich. We all gather up our bottles, gather around and toast the earth, toast each other, celebrate the harvest, and drink ourselves into a cider-induced coma.

Most of the men and women at the event are new to me, coming from all over the valley, and I don't see them again until the following year. I can't remember all the names, but I recall standing shoulder to shoulder with folks from a diverse spectrum of lifestyles, backgrounds, shapes and colors, a human mélange as equally diverse as the buckets of apples, human goodness squeezed out of us, blending effortlessly together, most of us deep into the autumns of our live, reflecting on all the journey's we have taken, bumpy roads we have endured, wrong turns leading to nowhere, all the buses we've missed, all the desperately devastating heartbreaks we experience.

Whatever challenges each one of us may be facing, whatever our burdens, whatever millstones we may have around our neck, we all take a pause for half a day, clean our filters, breathe in the aroma of the earth, the bounty of the season, where we are neither cured nor saved, where burdens may not be removed, but are briefly forgotten, and we walk away with very sore arms knowing there is always another season, another harvest, that the earth will keep on turning like the antique wooden apple press, and though our glass is cloudy, we see things a bit more clearly.

I think about my friend, Henry, in Mercer Island, a stranger at a bus stop, whose philosophy for living is the colorful coda of cider lovers everywhere. Apple cider: It may not give you a longer life, but it sure can't hurt.

(This chapter has been repurposed from a previous book I wrote. I felt it belonged here, with other thoughts about human challenges, and our amazing resiliency to overcome them.)

"YOU'LL NEVER SEE ALL
THE AWESOME THINGS
AHEAD OF YOU IF YOU KEEP
LOOKING AT ALL THE BAD THINGS
BEHIND YOU. SOMETIMES YOU
JUST HAVE TO TURN AROUND,
GIVE A LITTLE SMILE,
THROW THE MATCH
AND BURN THAT BRIDGE.
LIVE, LEARN, AND
DON'T LOOK BACK."

AUTHOR UNKNOWN

11
GOOD TIMBER

My wife and I are travelers, or for many years have been travelers. Not so much anymore. We've seen Rome, Paris, London, Moscow, Beijing, and a long list of many other cities around the globe. It turns out one of our favorite trips wasn't an exotic distant locale, rather, visiting New England in the fall. Maine is, without question, my pick for the most beautiful state in the country, with its rugged coastline, a national park, and the explosion of unearthly colors each October.

We love history and architecture; we love art and music, we love fashion and design; and we have seen all that Europe, the Pacific and Caribbean islands, Russia and China have to offer. On my office desk, I have a large chunk of the Berlin Wall that I chiseled off with my own hands, heeding the challenge of Ronald Regan: "Mr. Gorbachev, *tear down this wall.*"

Still, very near the top of my list of favorite sights: The massive hardwood forests of New England, old growth trees like maple, oak, beech, chestnut, sycamores and other silent and stately sentries that truly built this nation. I've heard it said that our hardwood forests were at one time so dense that a squirrel could travel from Bangor to Boston, or from Providence to Peoria without ever touching the ground. When you drive through the trees, hike historic trails made by deer, mice, caribou, and bears, when you spend time deep within the woods, it feels very possible that the squirrel story may be more than anecdotal.

And then it's back home to a desert. Scarcely a hardwood tree to be found. The contrast is glaring.

You have your favorite spots, too. Your idea of beauty will be different than mine. Aside from falling in love with New England forests, I still have a pine tree bias. I spent years vacationing in Idaho, Montana, Wyoming, and Utah's backcountry, fishing every river, stream, rivulet, and lake that I thought might yield up a rainbow, a brown or a cutthroat trout. A family cabin and the Caribou National Forest was a gathering spot for our family for half a century. Please forgive my Mountain West, pine tree bias.

It doesn't feel quite right to compare one beautiful place to another, your idea of beauty versus mine. That's a tough assignment and an argument that's hard to win. This missive is not about comparing. It's a celebration of trees, a love of trees, a respect for trees and their critical role in earth's hydrologic cycle. In my judgement trees represent cooperation, consistency, harmony, and balance. Trees are an appropriate symbol of living and working together, something that humans are not particularly good at these days. They also symbolize resiliency and stamina, surviving the harshest of conditions.

Wherever I have lived I have planted trees, dozens of trees, even in places where I knew that subsequent homeowners would benefit from the trees far more than I ever would. I like the notion that I was never simply planting trees. I was planting shade, I was planting fresh air, I was creating beauty.

Many years ago, I made a point of memorizing a poem that has become an integral part of my personal brand, a simple reminder about standing tall. It was written by Douglas Malloch, sometimes referred to as the "Lumbermen's Poet."

The tree that never had to fight
    For sun and sky and air and light,
But stood out in the open plain
    And always got its share of rain,
Never became a forest king
    But lived and died a scrubby thing.

The man who never had to toil
    To gain and farm his patch of soil,
Who never had to win his share
    Of sun and sky and light and air,
Never became a manly man
    But lived and died as he began.

Good timber does not grow with ease,
    The stronger wind, the stronger trees,
The further sky, the greater length,
    The more the storm, the more the strength.
By sun and cold, by rain and snow,
    In trees and men good timbers grow.

Where thickest lies the forest growth
    We find the patriarchs of both.
And they hold counsel with the stars
    Whose broken branches show the scars
Of many winds and much of strife.
    This is the common law of life.

Back to my pine tree bias for just a moment.

My long-time friend, Guy Morris, was at my home a couple of years ago, probably in 2021 when friends were reconnecting after the pandemic. Guy definitely has a pine tree bias. I have a dozen or so Colorado blue spruces and Austrian pines along the back edge of my acreage, lining Nebo Creek that runs through it. Guy noticed something. One of the spruces was missing its top. I knew it was missing its top, and I had already made plans to correct it, but I let Guy explain to me the consequences of topless evergreens, content to give him the spotlight and due credit.

In the forest, no one bothers with such things, but in the sprawls of suburbia, the crowded confines of concrete captivity, conifers must be well groomed, well shaped. If the broken top condition isn't rectified, your spruce will end up broader than it is tall. Not a good look, not at all in harmony with nature.

Another unacceptable malady found in concrete jungles, is a pine tree that has two tops. If left untreated both tops will keep growing, parallel to one another, creating a fork. Right now, you may look at it and think, "It looks fine to me." But in subsequent years, there may come a time in the life of the forked tree when either wind, snow, or lightening will split the tree from the fork all the way to the bottom. Two tops, if not corrected, is a certain death sentence for the tree.

Both anomalies can be fixed but it must be done in the early, formative years. In the case of the two-tops, simply cut one off. It rarely comes back, and the tree then puts its energy into the remaining top which will now be the leader, the captain of the journey to the sun.

And what of the tree that has, through no fault of its own, lost its leader. You simply go to the damaged area and find a branch just below the wound and promote it to captain. With a sturdy stake in the ground, tie the branch tenderly but firmly to the stake. The branch will bend. It will be flexible enough for you to make this adjustment without breaking it.

So, thanks to my friend, Guy Morris for his love of trees and his tender concern about each one of them. He left me with a few thoughts.

First, every tree counts whether in its native habitat or in your urban jungle where trees are far too scarce.

Second, you can never plant too many trees. They are good for the here and now, and even better for people who come after you. Let's plant more multi-generational shade.

Third, good timber doesn't grow with ease, but, just like everyone of us, it is through adversity that we grow strong.

Trees are great teachers, demonstrating each day, how to live in harmony, how to cooperate and work together in symbiotic relationships. How to get along.

It is estimated that there are 3.04 trillion trees worldwide*, up from just 750 billion a hundred years ago. Another way to put it is that there are 422 trees for every person on Earth. I don't know who counts them all, but that seems like good news, up a couple of trillion. It appears we have become and are becoming better and better stewards of trees and other natural resources. Despite global warming, we are learning, however slowly, how to be better caretakers of "the garden where His feet pass."

They are still cutting down rain forests in Brazil. Developers are still pulling up hill-side orchards, replacing them with houses that are prone to sliding into rivers. But despite these and other unforgivable practices, we are doing well. We are making progress. Don't let the hopelessly unreliable media mislead you.

Don't engage in climate debates with haughty politicians who know less about any of this than your third-grader. Instead plan a picnic and sit with a pretty girl on a blanket underneath the sycamore tree, look up into its branches, look beyond the branches into the heavens, into the stars, and remember that this forty-foot marvel was once a sapling or a seedling that pushed through the storms, stood tall, stood firm just for you and the tender, young saplings you nurture and leave behind.

"THE TRUE MEANING OF LIFE
IS TO PLANT TREES
UNDER WHOSE SHADE
YOU DO NOT
EXPECT TO SIT."

NELSON HENDERSON

12
BUYING NEW TIRES

I was shopping for new tires one Saturday afternoon, a task that has always been tedious and challenging for me. I know nothing about them and, fortunately, I haven't had to do it very often. A very nice young salesman approached me. I wanted to ask him about tread design, or inner wall construction, but couldn't think of anything to ask him without giving away how dumb I really was.

"I can make this simple," I said. "I need four new, high-quality tires at a price that won't break the bank."

I indicated to him that my car came from the factory with Michelin tires, a brand I've always thought of as one of the best. I asked him, "Should I stay with Michelin's? Do you have some in stock?"

His answer, "To be honest, you don't need Michelin tires. We don't stock them because we have found any number of alternatives that are just as good. Michelin tires are way too pricey for most buyers but let me show you what I think will work for you."

The guys that work in tire stores always have dirty hands, blackened by wrestling rubber all day. It's a dirty business and I wondered if he had been trained in anything other than the dirty side of the business. I wondered if they had any real salesmen. It didn't matter one way or the other, this guy was a real tire expert. He quickly recommended four high-quality tires at a fair price, and I felt good about his suggestion.

Everything about your car feels better when you drive on brand new tires, carefully balanced and inflated, making a reassuring and comforting hum as you head on down the road. There's a certain confidence you feel driving on new tires.

As I was making my way back home, I thought about something the salesman said. Nothing specifically about tires, their features, their advantages, rather a colloquial phrase we have come to use in our day-to-day conversations: "To be honest with you….."

As I said, he was very good and earned my trust immediately. I wondered if I felt he was honest because he started the conversation by telling me he was honest.

There is a slight variation on the phrase. Listen carefully, lots of people will say to you, "Do you want me to be honest with you?" How do you answer that. "No, I much prefer lying to honesty. Please tell me a pack of lies."

Next time someone asks for my permission to be honest, my answer is going to be, "Yes, please. I am hereby granting you permission to be honest with me. From this moment on you don't need to ask me. Just give me the truth. Assume I will always want the truth."

And then there is this: "Can I be perfectly honest with you?" Now we've moved past regular honesty and into the realm of perfect honesty. Is there any other kind of honesty? Do we need to modify it with "perfect?" Isn't truth, always perfect. If it isn't perfect, if there are shades of gray, then it isn't truth.

I have a very close friend of more than forty-years, someone I met in my days working in the political arena. Frequently, when asked a question he begins his answer this way: "Truth be told."

I'm pretty sure he isn't aware he's saying this, a phrase he likely picked up in the small town where he grew up. Interesting that the political arena is where you are least likely to find someone who begins every sentence with "truth be told."

Now that I have this curious little phrase in my head, I have started to hear it much more often than I used to. It's probably been around as part of our lexicon for many years, I'm just now more aware of how often it is used.

There are other similar, what I will call "red flag" figures of speech. Here's one:

"I don't mean to be critical, but..... When someone prefaces their comment with this, it's a warning. They are about to be critical.

Here's another:

"I don't want to interrupt, but".....the minute this comes out of their mouth, you have been interrupted.

"I don't mean to change the subject, but"…that's exactly what they just did.

"I don't mean to talk behind their back, but"..... Be assured, you are about to hear something gossipy.

"It goes without saying"….Then why are you saying anything?

You use these phrases all the time. Admit it. We all do because we somehow always want to set expectations and prevent backlash and blame. I believe in the basic goodness of man, and our intrinsic longing to love and be loved, to be seen and thought of as fair, trustworthy, respected, fair to others. We don't want our reptations sullied and tarnished by lies, innuendo, and hurtful gossip.

The hardest thing we face is being honest with ourselves because it frequently means admitting defeat and failure. My son recently stepped down as the CEO of a technology company because he no longer felt comfortable telling investors and customers that his products would be a massive improvement for their industry. He knew they never would. He made a conscious choice to be honest. His decision was not a great career decision, it was an extremely tough economic decision, but it was the right decision, the morally right thing to do.

It is so easy to lie. Most of the time you never get caught. It's very, very hard to be honest all the time. It takes a concerted effort.

I want to hear the news media begin every broadcast with the news anchors proclaiming, "Tonight we're going to be perfectly honest with you." And all the reporters rally around the journalistic pledge as they begin their reportage, "Truth be told."

I don't want you to tell me you are honest, just be honest. I'll recognize it.

How would it be If a stand-up comic begins his set by telling us how funny he is. Don't tell me how funny you are, just make me laugh.

What if the President of the U.S. begins a press conferences, asking the nation, "Can I be honest with you?" Yes, please Mister president, we're begging you to be honest. From now on you have permission from the American public to be honest.

At this writing I have two granddaughters graduating from high school, both off to college, two others already in their junior year. They are at the stage in their lives when they are mature enough to spot the cheaters, the liars, the hypocrites, the backstabbers, and begin to understand who their true friends really are, you know, those who stand by you regardless of circumstance. They are savvy enough to recognize the immature girls who flit from group to group hoping to be liked and admired by others, willing to do anything to succeed, fickle, untrustworthy, clueless about hurting feelings, caught up in the modern vortex of social media which, in the end, is an anti-social medium.

I've always believed that teenagers eventually outgrow their fickleness. I'm not so sure anymore. In the age of digital selfishness, "being seen just to be seen," they are turning from needy teenage narcissists into needy adult narcissists who can never get enough adulation and admiration.

My gang of grands, and your young sons and daughters, will need authenticity from the people around them, an easy offset to abundant phoniness. And they will need honesty as they seek clarity and understanding in their new, challenging environments.

My grandmother and my mother always reminded me that "Honesty is the best policy." I remember wondering "what is the second-best policy?"

These new scholars are heading down the road of infinite possibilities toward a million different diverse dreams. They'll need much more in the way of guidance than they know right now. And they'll continue to need maps and milestones along the way to measure their forward progress. They'll need new tires, occasionally, treads of their shoes like the treads on rubber tires, eventually wearing thin from wandering off course and making too many wrong turns. What they don't need is parents, friends, business colleagues and others asking them, "Do you want me to be honest with you?" It should be understood that they just want and expect everyone to be honest. Perfectly honest.

"HONESTY IS SUCH
A LONELY WORD,
AND MOSTLY WHAT
I NEED FROM YOU."

BILLY JOEL

13
A VIEW FROM THE PRAIRIE

spent some time working in Canada once as a young man, later servicing a couple of tech companies that had hired my firm to do their marketing and advertising. I have spent time in Vancouver, British Columbia, Calgary and Edmonton, Alberta, and Saskatoon Saskatchewan. I helped manage a very large conference for a client in Toronto, and I have vacationed with family in Montreal, Quebec.

I don't claim to have seen the entire country, and I've been in just a handful of cities. But I've been seen enough to have a sense for the breadth, the vastness, and the scope of the land. On many occasions I have mentioned to a number of people that Vancouver may be the prettiest city in North America.

Not quite so pretty, not quite as memorable, are the vast, endless miles of prairie with a horizon that goes on forever. I've heard it said, from locals and visitors alike, that out on the prairie you can stand on a tuna fish can and see the back of your head. It's flat out there.

I live in the Rocky Mountain West, in the shadow of towering peaks, but only about an hour away from the world-famous Bonneville Salt Flats, home to virtually every land speed record in the racing world.

The Prairies of Alberta are spectacularly beautiful compared to the desert just west of Salt Lake City, perhaps one of the ugliest places on earth. If not ugliest then certainly the most tragic, the bottom of an ancient dead sea where nothing ever grows.

Canada is a very young country, given Dominion status from Great Britain in 1867. The nation rapidly expanded, the Canadian Pacific Railroad expanded, the great rivers were harnessed, oil and gas were discovered, and the seemingly desolate plains blossomed into a prosperous country.

Still, it can seem barren, inhospitable, with a vastness that swallows you.

Turns out those prairies are the best place on earth to grow rapeseed, a member of the mustard family and the third-largest source of vegetable oil and the second-largest source of protein meal in the world. Canada is by far the largest grower of this valuable commodity. Worthless flatland? More like fields of gold, with a shocking yellow color painted in wide swaths by an artist gone mad.

The prairie has a beauty that is easy to overlook.

I found myself, one afternoon out on a long dusty road, about twenty miles south of Calgary. My client and I had spent the day in business meetings, and he invited me to his ranch for dinner. This was long before the advent of GPS. I followed his directions the best I could, keeping my finger on the map, inching my way along roads with very little directional signage, very rarely an intersection. Up ahead in the distance, I saw a shimmering light. My head grew weary, and my sight grew dim….. (No, no, sorry, I got mixed up. Those are lyrics from "Hotel California.) What I did see, up ahead in the distance, was someone standing by a mailbox. "Good grief,"

I thought. "There is life out here after all. Saints be praised."

I stopped to ask for directions. Despite the fact that this guy owned and farmed about a billion acres, he knew my client, his neighbor, and knew exactly how to get to his ranch.

"Stay south on this road," he explained, "for two eye-seeings, then head east for one more eye seeing. You'll be right in front of his place."

"Okey Dokey. Great. Sounds good," I sputtered. "I'm sorry, just one other tiny question: can you tell me what an 'eye-seeing' is?"

He looked incredulous, assuming that everyone knew what an eye-seeing is. "Look down that road," he prompted. I obeyed. "Keep looking. Do you see where the road disappears?" That's an eye-seeing.

"There's not much in the way of landmarks, or visual markers out there," I said, trying to comprehend.

"Just the horizon." he deadpanned. "That's a pretty big marker."

I thanked him and drove off, focusing on that first imaginary point. Don't blink. Don't breathe. Keep focused. I made it to what I thought was one eye-seeing, got out of my rental car and stood in the middle of the road trying to find the second one, then set off, wondering how ancient mariners sailed the seas with only the stars to guide them across a flatness far vaster than Alberta, Canada. I started feeling like I needed a sextant because I was going to be stuck out there all night. But this was a summer evening, and I wouldn't see stars for several more hours up here in the land of the midnight sun. I heard that creepy little music from "The Twilight Zone" playing in my ear.

I had no idea how far I'd gone. I decided to turn around and got to that mailbox where I'd started and try again. The farmer was still standing there with his hands in his pockets.

"You went too far," he pronounced. He pretty much knew I would be back.

My head was on the steering wheel, afraid to look him in the eye. He opened the passenger door and climbed in beside me. "Let's go," he commanded. "I'll show you. I'll have one of the boys drive me back."

I'm going to compress the story from here. We got to my appointment, and I got back to Calgary without any more problems, hopped on a plane the next morning and vowed to better understand the notion of "eye-seeings."

It's been twenty-plus years and I still haven't mastered it like the farmer at the mailbox, perfectly at home with endlessness. The only conclusion I can reach is that certain people must be better at looking down the road than me. Perhaps there is a host of people endowed with some brain mechanism that allows them to see the horizon. And beyond.

I'm just not one of them.

Most of my adult life I've set goals, dreamed big, and have concocted schemes, many of them successful, guided by something my father taught me: "He aims too low who aims beneath the stars."

But someone else said to me, recently, "The Devil is in the future," meaning you'll go crazy thinking about the future because you can neither see it, predict it or control it. The anthem of this sect might well be a song from the '60s group Grass Roots, "Sha Na Na Na Na Na, live for today, and don't worry 'bout tomorrow heyyyy."

Writers, philosophers, spiritualists, psychologists, better trained in existentialism than me, have, for eons examined, elucidated and expounded on these two sides of the coin. Lean into the future with gusto, goals, and dreams. Or live strictly in the moment, maximizing the here and now.

I'd capsulize the debate this way: It's either come what may or get out of the way.

No one has articulated any of this better than Carrie Watts the lead character in the film "The Trip to Bountiful" written by the incredible Academy award winning Horton Foote. Carrie is living in a cramped apartment with her son and his annoying wife, hoping to see "Bountiful" her childhood home in Texas one last time. Her son refuses to take her, doubting that "Bountiful" even exists anymore. Carrie sneaks out, and with the help of a stranger, takes a bus ride back home, discovering that it has indeed disappeared with age. During the entire trip she sings hymns, which her daughter-in-law thinks are out of date, and talks to her new friend about her regrets and disappointments, wishing things had worked out differently.

Coming to grips with it all she laments, "I guess the Lord made the earth round so we can't see too far down the road."

There is a bit of Carrie Watts in each of us, seeking clarity while hoping to avoid decay. It would be nice to stand on a tuna fish can and see into forever, or at the very least to reach a few eye seeings every now and then. I'll bet you have wished, just as I have, many times, to know what's ahead and it drives you crazy because you can't control it, plan for it, and you have to make decisions in a void.

You know what I want to tell my children, my grandchildren, and now my very first great-grandson, Rocky? I want to tell them to charge into tomorrow, to know that horizons aren't fences, they are gateways. Run as fast as you can into the future.

Yet, as I begin to decay and fade away, I've grown increasingly comfortable with the "live in the moment" philosophy. What do you think? In which camp do you pitch your tent?

Happy in hoping, or sad for settling?

Carpe Diem, seize the day, live in the moment. Or "Just think of the possibilities."

It's impossible to know what's out there without first knowing what's in you. Spend some quality time with yourself, understanding who you are and, define yourself on your terms not on the expectations of others.

I remember being dazzled when a third-grade teacher brought in an artist who taught us how do draw perspective. You start by placing a dot on the paper which becomes a vanishing point. I would sit for hours drawing telephone poles, fences, big city skyscrapers, and the white painted stripes on the highway, disappearing at the vanishing point. I was fascinated by what may exist, just beyond the vanishing point.

I learned something in Canada. The prairies aren't barren, they're beautiful, and full of a richness you can't see. They aren't a wasteland; they are a wonderland. Step out onto your personal flat, endless prairie, look past the barrenness and see if you can find a little hope, balance, and a new perspective. They are out there.

Come on up. I'll be there with the farmer at his mailbox, up on the flatlands of Alberta, urging you on.

"PREDICTION IS VERY DIFFICULT, ESPECIALLY ABOUT THE FUTURE."

NIELS BOHR

14
LOOKING AHEAD

It feels worthwhile to take a moment and recall the title of this book, **"Milestones and Millstones."** It's about looking forward to great things, Milestones guiding us along the road, always making progress. But it's also about giant stones around our necks, weighing us down, holding us back.

In virtually all of our endeavors, it seems we're either looking forward, or we're looking back. This is the natural and normal way of the human brain.

Any number of great thinkers have referenced the concept of always looking forward. Abraham Lincoln opined, "The best way to predict the future is to make it."

There are two other directions that may instruct us. One is up, the other is down.

I'm not sure where heaven is, but when we speak about it, wonder about it, we always look up, up to the sky, up to the stars. The vastness immediately overwhelms you and you get a glimpse of eternity. I highly recommend looking up.

We may also spend a lot of time looking down, typically not a great habit. Sad people look down a lot, never looking others in the eye. These individuals may be afraid of what's ahead, mired in the darkness of their past, their disasters and disappointments, their tragedies, their traumas, their remorse, regrets, and retributions.

Still, I believe that looking down, occasionally, has great benefits. Collecting shells along the beach. Walking the Freedom Trail in Boston, following the line through the pages of history, stepping, literally, in the footsteps of our ancestors. Hiking through a forest, looking for mushrooms or berries. Making an errant shot in golf, hunting for that miserable little white ball.

Generally speaking, looking down can be perilous. You may miss a crosswalk, fail to see oncoming cars and get run over by a bus.

I know two very serious down-lookers, committed to always looking down. They have proved it's a worthwhile thing to do. Karen Eades and her mother Wanda McIntosh, got together every morning for a brisk walk and a great aerobic workout. It was also a chance for mother and daughter to connect and stay in touch.

They never got too far from home, following the sidewalks in their suburban neighborhood, around the church parking lot, cut through the gas station, past a few shops and one or two restaurants.

For some thirty years, these two intrepid suburban saunterers, these sidewalk sleuths, with eyes always down, collected lost coins, a nickel here, a quarter there, and lots of worthless, nearly obsolete pennies.

Wanda died a few years ago, and her family gathered together to count her coins. They filled five orange **Home Depot** plastic buckets to the brim with the coins. Each bucket totaled $1,200. Wanda's wandering had yielded about $6,000.

The five siblings spent a few moments examining the contents. A few of the coins were coated in tar and oil. They had been stuck in the highway at some point, and Wanda would get down on her hands and knees, if necessary, dig them out with a screwdriver and toss them on the pile, didn't matter how filthy it was. A lost coin is a lost coin.

She would also check every soda pop machine and every telephone-booth coin return box (ask your parents what those things are), frequently finding a coin or two that someone forgot to retrieve. It became ridiculous, and family members pretended not to know her, when one day on a road trip, she went hunting for coins in every possible place at a truck stop near Fresno, California. She looked so earnest, almost desperate to find a coin, that a good Samaritan, thinking Wanda was homeless, handed her a $20 bill. The siblings happily took their share of Wanda's coins in the buckets, but none of them would touch the ill-gotten $20 bill.

Wanda thought she was just picking up coins. What she was really doing was creating a manifesto about moving, about progress through perseverance. And Wanda, no doubt, would have learned that there is wealth, there are valuable gems to be found, wherever we go. Even in gutters.

I have come to believe that we can find just about anything we're looking for. We can go looking for misery, it's everywhere. And we can find joy and happiness if we sincerely, diligently and constantly seek it, pick it up, embrace it, internalize it. When you do this over and over and over, scientists tell us your malleable brain will become a more joyful brain.

Wanda found a lot of coins each time she walked, but it was never about money. The discovery that made her rich, was spending time with her daughter, a coin of inestimable value.

Wanda would love these words from an unknown author: "Looking back gives you regrets. Looking ahead gives you opportunity."

Wanda the wanderer, thank you so much for your example

and your wise advice. It's surprising what you find simply by continually moving your feet, propelling you forward, getting up, getting out, getting off your saggy old couch of regrets, putting on your shoes of hope, your jacket of optimism, your glasses of vision, and start walking. You never know what you may discover.

You may be the kind of person who wakes up each morning to a foggy, fuzzy view of the world through the sometimes desperate eyes of pessimism and depondence. But, you can choose a clearer perspective by looking at the world through Wanda's eyes, gazing at her wide vista of endless possibilities and opportunities right in front of you.

I will no longer take morning walks for exercise. But, I will still rise early, put on good shoes and take a "Wanda." If you need to find me, I'll be down at the covered bridge waiting for you. You're welcome to come "Wanda" with me.

15
NO SOLICITING

(1961, probably)

The doorbell rings. My younger brother, Reed, dashes to the door, a cocker spaniel on his heels. Standing there on the stoop is a young man, probably late twenties. He is wearing a tweed jacket and bowtie making him look more professorial than salesman. I remember, clearly that it was July, about a hundred degrees outside, and this guy is in a tweed jacket, dripping with sweat.

His hand is perched on a shiny, new, Kirby vacuum, and he is grinning from ear to ear.

"Hey there young fella," he says to Reed. "I've got something here I think you would like to see. Is your mother here?"

"Yes."

"You think I could come in for a few moments. It's really hot today, isn't it. If I could just come in out of the heat….."

We had a strict policy at our house. No salesmen. Ever. Reed knew this but the Kirby team is well trained in the art of getting in the door, and he pushed right past Reed who has dashed into the kitchen to tell Mom. "Mom, there's a guy here selling vacuums. He wants to show it to you."

"Reed," she replies. "We have a policy around here, no salesmen. Have you forgotten the policy. I don't need another vacuum, go back in there and ask him to leave."

"Mom," Reed pleads, "just go talk to him. I can't go ask him to leave. It's so hot and he's sweating like a pig."

"Hey, we're all hot. It's July." And then she stormed into the living room, a couple of .45 caliber guns strapped to her hips. A bull-whip hangs from her apron. Reed sprints all over the house and the yard, gathering three other Hurst boys, including me.

"Guys come with me, right now," he orders. "There's a sales guy at the door and mom is just about to put on a show."

Within seconds, four boys, (all of them born in a five-year span) wearing basically the same striped t-shirts from J.C. Penny's, blonde hair completely shaved for the summer, plop down on the floor just as the show begins.

The salesman has already dumped dirt, cat hair, some thumbtacks, sawdust, and Cheerios on the carpet. Oh, and a bowling ball.

Mom walks in, "What are you doing? I don't need a vacuum, thank you very much for coming. I have a lot of work to do. Goodbye."

"OK, no problem," Mr. overzealous Kirby, says." "Let me just clean up this mess first."

This is exactly how the Kirby vacuum company operates. Get in the house, make a mess, then demonstrate the power of their latest model. Mr. Bowtie starts to remove his jacket. A non-verbal glare from mom says don't even think about it.

He presents his business card with a slight bow, as if he is being introduced to the pope or Queen Elizabeth. "Roger Davies, at your service. And you are Mrs.???

"Just clean up the mess, Roger."

We were dazzled by the demonstration. The dirt was gone, the sawdust disappeared, thumbtacks rattled through the rollers, and the mess vanished in an instant."

Caught up in the moment I said, "Mom that is a really good

vacuum. You should get it." I learned a lot about Mom's non-verbal glare in that moment and I would spend the next dozen years looking down, trying not to ever make eye contact with her again.

The bowling ball still sits there. Roger looks at the four of us. "Boys you want to pick up this bowling ball?" Oldest brother Brent volunteers to give it a try. "Twelve pounds," Roger says.

Roger quickly attaches an additional wand to the vacuum, and it is now a multi-functional house-hold marvel that helps you clean the curtains, the dust bunnies under the beds, anything that needs cleaning.

He walks over to the ball, the grand finale, puts an inverted suction cup on the round nozzle of the hose on it, and effortlessly picks up the heavy resin ball. Mom is not impressed.

"Mrs. Hurst, I want to sell you this vacuum today and I'm authorized to give you a twenty-five-dollar discount. But that offer is only good for today. And one other thing, if I sell just one more vacuum, I will have hit my quota and earn a trip to Hawaii."

"You've met your quota?" Mom queries.

"Yes. Just as soon as I make this sale with you," Roger says, proudly.

"Okay. Let me see if I've got this straight, Mom begins. Four little boys are now disappearing under chairs and behind the curtains.

She continues the interrogation, "So, I buy a vacuum I don't need, and you jet off to Hawaii while I stay here and vacuum floors all day, picking up all the bowling balls scattered around the house."

"That's not what I'm saying," Roger stammers.

"I'm pretty sure that's exactly what you are saying," Mom

counters. "You go to the beach, I go to the grocery store. You get a surfboard, I get an ironing board."

Roger seals his fate. "But you're getting a much better clean."

"So, I'm not a good housewife and you're here to help me? Is that right?"

"This is the very best vacuum the Kirby company has ever made," Roger says beaming. (Any good salesperson uses this tactic known as deflecting. Don't answer the question.)

"Quick question," Mom says. "How much does this thing weigh? It feels very heavy?"

"It is heavier than most other vacuums on the market," Roger concedes, "because it is the sturdiest machine on the market. Sturdier means stronger. It is so well built that you'll be using this baby for the next thirty years."

Four little boys simultaneously moan, "Buy the vacuum, mom. Please just buy the vacuum before this gets bloody."

"Wow," mom says. "Vacuuming for thirty years. That sounds great. How many trips to Hawaii do you think you'll earn in the next thirty years?"

"A lot. I hope."

"This sounds like a very fair arrangement," mom says, surprising us all.

"I know," says the monumentally clueless salesman. "The Kirby vacuum company treats their sales team members really well."

"Well, that's really something," Mom says in a voice that sounds reassuring. "Hey, do they have any openings at the Kirby vacuum company? Here's what I'm thinking. If I become a Kirby team member, I could sell enough vacuums and earn a trip to Hawaii, and I wouldn't have to buy a vacuum from you. Who could I talk to about that, Roger?"

Roger looks like someone turned a fire hose on him, completely bathed in sweat, now mixed with a little blood coming out his pores.

Mom begins twisting the knife between his ribs. "Just write down the name and phone number of your boss right here. Then I can give him a call and join the team right away."

"So, you're not going to buy from me today? I mean my Hawaii trip and all..." Roger's voice trailed off.

"Oh no," mom chuckles. I never had any intention of buying one. I may have mentioned I don't need a vacuum. But I look forward to seeing you at the next sales training meeting. Do they have trophies for salesperson of the year? Or just the trips to Hawaii?

Mom is now holding the door open. "Thanks so much for coming."

Reed, who has by now slithered out of the room, beckons to me, "what's happening?"

"She's throwing him out," I tell him. "She's had her fun."

Lynn, the youngest of the four, hollers from behind the curtains. "Mom shut the door. Get this over with. You've made your point. Please shut the door."

Roger Davies strains to pick up the most poorly designed machine in history. He fumbles around trying to get his bag full of dirt and cat hair, and his ridiculous one-ton machine into his car. The vacuum slips from his grasp and lands on his foot. There is an audible crunch.

I learned a completely new vocabulary right then from a Kirby vacuum sales guy.

My dad made a living as a sales guy. Never door-to-door, but managed a team of reputable guys selling important new technological washing machines, dryers, refrigerators and freezers, television sets, stereos, and, later microwave ovens, you know things that really lighten the burdens of a home-maker. My mom loved her automatic dish washer, and boasted about the microwave oven and how it saved her so much time. In the early sixties these new appliances were a big deal.

Visitors would come from all over the neighborhood be-cause we had the first color tv, the latest stereos, gleaming white side-by-side washer and dryer sets. And we had an automatic ice cube maker. Kids would come over asking for a drink just to see the half round cubes pushed out of their molds, in the Whirl-pool miracle machine.

And my mom had clearly learned a little about sales tech-niques from a master sales guy. She used this knowledge as a spear gun which she now had pointed right between Roger Davies' eyes.

I remember her saying to Roger, just as he was about to drive away, "Roger, I hope you get to Hawaii. Good luck. Now, I'm going to tell you, very quickly, how to close a sale. Are you listening? Don't tell me what it will do for you. Tell me what it will do for me."

Roger unwisely opens his mouth, "Well I told you'd have a cleaner home."

"Yes you did. That's why I am now going to pull the trigger on this harpoon."

Again, mom repeats. "Tell me how it will change my life for the better, not change yours."

My mom was tough. Very tough. We called her Sarge, and she was very strict. She had a perpetual scowl on her face, the corners of her mouth dragged down by the weight of raising six kids, all of us just about as strong willed as she was.

"Oh, wait a minute," she says, pounding on Roger's Studebaker, second on the list of the worst designs in history. "When you get to Hawaii, could you send me a post card with a little hula skirt on it. That would be something I could really show my neighbors.

"And thanks for stopping by to hang your four-hundred-pound millstone around my neck, reminding me just how miserable housewives are."

This story is very close to being 90% true. I've colored it up just a bit. Mom was never particularly good with sarcasm, or humor, or irony so I may have put a few words in her mouth to help make a few points. She was always pretty direct with her feelings. Unmistakably clear.

But we did indeed witness the massacre at 811 East that hot day in July, and how she made Roger Davies sweat and squirm. I don't remember ever having another salesman in our house.

And I recall, many years later, the beginning of my education that day, not just about the art of selling, not simply how to close a sale, or clean a floor, but I learned that in any human relationship, it is so easy to be judgmental, to be dismissive, to be critical, to see someone else's world through your eyes only, failing to take the time to look into their eyes, see their pain and their needs, to listen to their story, to read their emotions, and recognize the burdens some people are asked to carry around. It takes a lifetime of practice, understanding others, but you'll get it. And when you do, you'll feel the undeniable power of asking the most important question in human relationships: "What can I do for you?"

Mom would eventually make it to Hawaii. In all I think she and dad went over six or seven times, maybe more. Dad organized the trips, and took his top sales guys and their wives, an incentive, and a reward for their hard work. I think each of my siblings will recall hearing about our parents' love of the islands, where they ate a lot of pineapple, soaked in a lot of sun, and completely embraced the casual laid back lifestyle of a people who were never in a hurry, where there are no sales quotas, no hectic schedules, no worries, and no floors to vacuum.

Completely worthless author's notes:

1-**Kirby Vacuum's Slogan**, "Helping customers clean with confidence for more than 100 years." First this feels like it belongs in the dangling participle bin. Am I going to be cleaning for the next 100 years? Second, I'm not sure women want to clean with confidence. They want to clean with ease, or they don't want to clean at all.

2-**I read a couple of reviews and spotted this**: If there's one small downside to using a Kirby vacuum, it's the sheer size of the device. This makes Kirby's amazing suction possible, but a weight of 23.3 pounds will definitely give some consumers pause.

The latest Kirby g4 is just shy of thirty pounds.

By contrast, the new Dyson vacuums weigh just 14 pounds, and glide around effortlessly on a ball that pivots, floats, and turns with just a slight twist of the wrist. My personal bias is showing here.

3-**Picking up a bowling ball**: Any vacuum can pick up a bowling ball when you put an inverted suction cup on the hose. I got this information from a very small vacuum manufacturer, Ristenbatt, which pulled back the curtain on this crafty bit of sales legerdemain. "Often, when analyzed with a few basic laws of physics in mind, these amazing feats prove very little and are relatively meaningless!"

4-**Finally, I acknowledge that this story focuses on women**, and it would be easy to assume I believe women should do all the cleaning. I believe no such thing. I regularly do household chores, cooking, scrubbing toilets, and I frequently vacuum half of the house. I take care of the downstairs. My wife does the upstairs. Men everywhere, I acknowledge your efforts and welcome you to the club of men, women and children who detest cleaning, and I grant you permission to constantly complain about it. Gripe all you want.

JUST MAKE SURE YOU GET IT DONE!

"YOU NEVER REALLY UNDERSTAND A PERSON UNTIL YOU CONSIDER THINGS FROM HIS POINT OF VIEW."

HARPER LEE

16
THE HUNGARIAN CLOCK

"Is this your bag, sir?" A very serious man in uniform was speaking to me.

"Yes."

"Please get bag and come with me."

"What's this about?" I asked him.

"Please get bag. Come with me," he repeats more firmly.

This is at the end of a trip to Europe, and we are standing in the security line at the airport in Budapest, Hungary, named for the famous Hungarian composer Franz Liszt. This is not how we wanted to end our two-week quest to see countries formerly behind the Iron Curtain. Our last stop was Budapest.

We had spent an exhausting five days exploring this remarkable city, taking a dip in the world famous Szechenyi thermal baths, cruising down the Danube, touring the spectacular parliament building, and riding the funicular up to Buda castle.

But, even with so much rich history and architecture, you would find it odd that our first stop in Budapest was a flea market on the edge of town. We had discovered that three or four couples traveling with us were antique enthusiasts, passionate packrats of the past, just like my wife and me, so we joined up with them and set off. The hotel concierge said taxis don't go out that far and suggested we take the subway.

No one in the group had ever been on a subway, a bunch

of westerners who love their cars. I have been on subways in London, Moscow, Stockholm and other European cities. In the U.S. I have navigated subways in New York, Chicago, Atlanta, and others including Washington D.C. where we lived for a time.

"It's easy," I tell them, reassuringly." "Here's the name of the area where we are going, and here's the name of the stop where we get off. We want this red-loop," I say, drawing my finger along the map, "heading east. The end of the line tells us which direction to go."

Three minutes later we are on the red-line train heading for some neighborhood with lots of c's, z's and barely one vowel in the name. Twenty minutes later we pop up into the sunlight, pretty much right in the middle of the flea market.

We immediately spotted a very old, small, children's teddy bear and we snatched it up without haggling on price. (Antiquing is all about haggling. Most sellers around the world play this charade, almost offended if you don't try to negotiate.)

Our team scatters, finding mostly worthless trinkets that antique addicts see as treasures. Lots of Russian remnants left behind, a silver stopwatch, a lady's hairbrush and mirror, a brass cigarette case, sepia toned photographs, brittle, cracking, yellowing, neglected, another two or three million victims of war.

And a clock.

It is a simple time piece that a family in the 1930's would typically place on a fireplace mantle. It doesn't appear to be a particularly expensive wood and is a very common shape with an arched curve, classic but uninspiring. But the clock was still ticking and came with the original key used to wind the springs.

I tried to haggle with the seller, but I proved to be an inept, ineffective negotiator. I have no idea what we paid for it, probably in the $25 dollar range. We loved its simplicity. We loved that it would add a historic touch to our eclectic décor.

Now it was time to pack our bags and head home. We were anxious to get home, sad that we ran out of time with still so many things to see. Our packing began with the clock, safely tucked into a cozy nest of dirty laundry, in the largest of three bags.

Then off to the airport and my encounter with the KGB or the Hungarian equivalent.

"Please, come with me," this unfriendly commandant orders for the third time. His name is probably something easy, like Smith, but on his official name tag I see "Schzchztgtachz."

I ask if there is any particular reason that the Hungarians have chosen not to use vowels. Did the Communists banish them?

He remains expressionless and taciturn.

I am essentially taken into police custody, escorted into a back room. I was hoping that all vestiges of Soviet gulags were gone and that I could get on the plane with my wife and the rest of our group, now boarding.

"Please open bag," I am ordered.

I comply, grab a zipper, and throw back the lid.

"Please, everything out."

"Unpack this bag? You can't be serious. (He was.) "Do you have any idea how long it takes my wife to pack a bag?" I say with a forced chuckle. "You can't believe how much stuff she needs just for her hair. You married, Mr. Schzchztgtachz? You know what I'm talking about, right?"

I get barely an eye roll. "And now you want me to take everything out?"

It looks like this guy has never heard of sarcasm. I think the communists also banished humor. And smiles. And personalities.

I start pulling out pants and shirts, followed by a bunch of dirty laundry. I ask Mr. Schzchztgtachz if most travelers take time to wash laundry before packing, or, like us just chuck it in dirty.

"Remove everything from bag, quickly." He seems grossed out by the dirty jockey shorts.

Then, the clock. A clock that looked suspiciously like a bomb as it passed through the X-ray scanner.

An entire battalion of security agents gather around, hands on their holsters. "What is this?" I'm asked.

"Ahhh, It's a clock?" My inflection goes up at the end, like a question.

"I know what clock is. Where you get? Why you have clock in suitcase? Do they not have wrist watches in U.S?

He tosses back a little sarcasm, but still no smile.

The fifty or so people we've been traveling with are now on the plane. My wife is with them. They are ready to close the doors and prepare for take-off, and still I'm in the back room being interrogated by the gestapo, frantically trying to shove everything back in the suitcase. A dirty piece of underwear goes flying and no one moves.

Tick tock tick tock tick tock. The new Hungarian clock joins the chorus of other clocks in our house, all speaking the universal language of time, the rhythm of the earth. It sat on the mantle of our fireplace for about twelve years, about which time we left the city and moved to farm country. Somewhere in the move we lost the key to the Hungarian clock. You might say time stopped.

There is a small door on the back of the clock that enables you to see the inner workings and change the volume of the hourly chime. While preparing for the move I remember taking the time to tape the key inside the clock for safe keeping. I was certain I took this precaution.

Still, it was nowhere to be found.

The clock survived a Russian invasion, the ignominy of being sold at a flea market very little haggling over the price, and ended up in the hands of a guy who is either lazy, or monumentally inept, and lost the key.

I had imagined the very real possibility that the clock could have blood on its hands, taken by the Nazi's from a humble Jewish home, then deserted, forgotten. I began blocking out a story, believing I could write a compelling novel about a secret slot inside the clock where the original owner, a jeweler, had hidden the key to a bank security box. I would find the bank, take the key and open it, discovering a stash of diamonds and rubies. In my story I'd make a lifetime, heroic effort to reunite the clock and the priceless gems, with the rightful owners. I'm sort of, kinda, still thinking about writing that novel.

With no key to wind it, we put the tragic, little clock on top of a dresser in the back bedroom, where we never go, and it sat there, completely inert and silent for six years. A daughter came from Texas for a visit and noticed the lifeless lump. She wondered if it was broken. Could it be fixed?

"What clock?" I puzzled.

"The one you brought from Europe a long time ago."

The clock that nearly got me banished to a Siberian jail, the clock that we proudly rescued from the pages of history, had been forgotten. The lack of a key had rendered it worthless, in my mind. I had given up any hope that I could find the exact key, for that exact clock, which made its way from Budapest to Salt Lake City, then up to the cottage in the mountains of Northern Utah. How could I possibly find that exact key.

I didn't know where to begin looking so, where does everything begin nowadays? (In farm country we use colloquialisms like nowadays instead of "in today's digital age.")

Click on Google.

I ended up on EBay where I found hundreds and hundreds of these things, usually called clock keys, or cranks, which came from old cranks used to wind Grandfather clocks. Hmmmmm. Grandfather and crank used in the same sentence, one used to get the other going. I don't like this conversation.

I carefully made a measurement inside the small keyhole and couldn't decide exactly which size I needed. Then I found a very large web site of a company called "Clockworks," and they had everything you could possibly need to keep clocks running. Even very old Hungarian Clocks. I found my answer: A universal key.

For six dollars I bought one. It's a universal key with five different sprockets, confident that one of the five would work. It did. The brass, star shaped device wound up the sleeping clock in short order. I set the hands to the correct time. And waited. And waited for it to start ticking. Nothing.

I opened the little door in the back to see if there were any other problems, and with just that small movement, the clock suddenly started ticking. You have to start the pendulum swinging, genius. A very simple movement. As long as the springs are tight, as long as you regularly wind the clock to keep the springs tight, the clock keeps time with its cousins elsewhere in our house.

From time to time, it lags behind the younger more modern clocks, so I just give a gentle nudge to the big hand, two minutes forward most of the time.

Don't you wish you could control time like that? Don't you dream of resetting the clock, forward or back, granting yourself a do-over? In the event you have too much time on your hands, or too little, you now have a key in your hands and the power to move the hands of the clock around the face, to any time you want. You control time. For a moment or two you are as powerful as any force in the universe. Set the hands to whatever time you want, then start the pendulum swinging again. You can wind it once a week and keep it ticking or ignore it at let time stand still.

Set the clock back a few minutes or a few years, and remember the times, the people, the events that brought you true happiness and joy. The more you go searching for joy, the more you find it, and eventually, your brain won't know if you are actually experiencing a moment of joy or just thinking about it. You have created a pathway in your brain, you have trained your brain to bring you joy, and to feel the emotions connected to those moments.

You are a powerful force in the universe because you can control time and you can rewire brains. But far more powerful than either of these, you have the ability to create joy.

And some of us, carrying around feelings of guilt, feelings of inferiority, failure, fear, or the pain of broken hearts, broken human connections, loss, tragedy and the ability to forgive oneself, I have something for you.

It's a universal key. We are all the same, and we all move forward to the same beat, and we all have weight on our shoulders and millstones around our necks. And we can, each of us, wind the springs tight again, start the pendulum swinging again, every now and then nudging the big hand forward or back by a minute or two as needed, listening to the steady cadence that reminds you that you are in charge of things.

You control time, and you are the final arbiter of joy, where to find it, and how to live it. You are master of the universe!

Tick tock tick tock tick tock…

"THE BAD NEWS IS
THAT TIME FLIES.
THE GOOD NEWS IS
YOU'RE THE PILOT."

MICHAEL ALTSHULER

17
FIND A PENNY

I was running errands and needed to stop at a local, one-stop, print shop. I opened the car door, stepped out and saw five pennies on the ground. I didn't move my feet, pulled my phone/camera out of my pocket, pointed it down at the ground, and snapped a photo.

I returned home and stared at the image, wondering three things.

First why did I bother taking this photo? What was it that caught my eye?

Second, how did five pennies end up there? Did someone accidentally drop them? Did someone toss them out the car window because the penny is worthless in today's economy?

Third, was it a sign of some sort, some puzzle, a secret coded message for a spy, part of a ritual of druids or aliens, perhaps a very small Stonehenge?

Somewhere deep in my memory bank I remembered a child's poem:

"Find a penny, pick it up,

And all day long you'll have good luck."

There are other versions of the lucky penny poem:

Find a penny leave it there, all the day you'll have despair.

Put the penny in your shoe, and good luck will come to you.

Give it to a faithful friend; then, your luck will never end.

Find a penny; let it lie, you'll need a penny before you die.

Whoa, that last one is a bit troubling!

Somewhere, somehow, the penny has become something of a universal symbol for luck. Add a four-leaf clover and a rabbit's foot and you have the triumvirate of talismans.

I personally rely on Lucky Charms cereal.

Using pennies as a symbol for luck, consider a few things.

Could the pennies have come from heaven? Does God mete out luck as he sees fit? At least one song writer believes he does.

Every time it rains, it rains

Pennies from Heaven

Don't you know each cloud contains

Pennies from Heaven?

You'll find your fortune falling all over town

Be sure that your umbrella is up, upside down.

There'll be pennies from heaven for you and me.

I distilled and synthesized my thoughts about the photo, about pennies, and in a much broader way, the concept of luck? Is it a real thing? Are some people luckier than others?

For thousands of years, every major culture has had a variety of ways to bring about luck, and included rituals, dances, magic potions. Each of these traditions was grounded in what we now think of as the supernatural, some unseen force in the universe from which these groups drew strength.

Of course, major religions still do this, but now it is in the form of prayer, fasting, self-denial, having faith in an unseen god who will answer our prayers.

I've been thinking about the difference between luck, superstitions, coincidence, and the hand of God moving pieces around a chess board, guiding our every move.

People define luck in three ways, according to Jacqueline Woolley, professor of psychology at the University of Texas at

Austin. She was quoted in a recent Wall Street Journal article.

"First, we often use the term luck as synonymous with "chance"; we may call it lucky to win at a slot machine, for instance, although it's actually a random event.

"Another way to frame luck is as a supernatural force that exists in the universe. This force may touch on different people at different times, and some people believe (or hope) it also can be harnessed, with a ritual or charm. (See Lucky Charms cereal above.)

"Third, it can be thought of as a personal trait: It's just something that you're born with."

Superstition is a belief or behavior that is considered irrational or supernatural.

Coincidence is a concurrence of events with no connection.

Then there is this curious concept known as the gambler's fallacy. It's this crazy way of denying the unpredictability of random events: "I haven't rolled a seven all week, so I'll definitely roll one tonight.

"Post hoc ergo propter hoc" is a fancy Latin way of explaining why things happen. It means "This, therefore because of that." A simple example is *"The rooster crows immediately before sunrise, therefore the rooster causes the sun to rise."*

These are not the thoughts of crazy people. Lots of important people practice rituals all the time.

Michael Jordan always wore his University of North Carolina practice shorts under his NBA uniform, believing that he won a championship because of them.

Tiger Woods, the greatest golfer in history has worn a red shirt in the final Sunday round of every major tournament since the moment he stepped on a professional course.

Red intimidates, it's a power color, and it's meant to instill fear in opponents' eyes. Seems to have worked out for Tiger.

Jack Nicklaus is also superstitious. He'll only golf when he has three coins in his pocket. The denomination doesn't matter, only the power of three. It apparently worked for him.

Kevin Garnett was a seven-foot monster who played 20 years in the NBA, making 15 All-Star Games. He had to eat at least one peanut butter-and-jelly sandwich before every game, a ritual his teammates on the Boston Celtics would also adapt.

Some of the most talented people in the world still don't entirely trust their talents. They lean on luck, on rituals, on good fortune, fate, destiny, what is written in the stars.

I heard a Hollywood actor once remark, "I went to Hollywood and caught a lucky break. It was fifteen years in the making." In other words, luck is most frequently tied to hard work.

I had a close encounter with the luck vs. talent conundrum. I had just sold my interest in an ad agency based in the San Francisco Bay area, and I had been invited to be the keynote speaker at a major symposium on how to create and build brands for emerging tech companies.

Sitting in the audience was the president of the San Francisco office of the largest marketing communications firm in the world. He asked me to come by his office. A week or so later I met with him, and he invited me to join the firm as Director of Brand Strategy, working with offices around the globe.

What a lucky break that he was in the audience that day. I felt so lucky to have been invited to speak at the conference! I couldn't believe my good fortune.

When Dan met with me in his office that day, he told me he had heard me speak elsewhere and came to the conference that day specifically to hear me. Luck had nothing to do with it. He admired my skills, my talent, my experience.

The Wall Street Journal article also offered this.

"People who are 'lucky' have a broader focus and they're more likely to encounter chance opportunities and then good things can happen. People who think of themselves as unlucky are just really sort of stuck in their narrow focus," the experts will tell you.

"What you can't expect is for good fortune to magically come your way without effort. Luck is a very big part of our self-identity, and isn't very malleable until you do something concrete about it."

Sometimes, everything seems to go wrong. You're passed over for a job. Your back aches. Your zipper breaks. Your cat keeps throwing up. Your new love interest ghosts you. You suddenly develop an allergy to dog hair--your own pet dog Fred. Faced with setbacks large and small, you feel like your life is always taking a turn for the worse. You aren't superstitious, but you begin to wonder — could you just be an unlucky person? Why does it seem like you can never catch a break?

Here's what I think. We make our own luck, good or bad by the way we think about ourselves and the way we go about daily activities.

So is luck a real thing? Considering yourself lucky or unlucky is a way of seeing yourself which then has impact on how you behave and how you think, and it becomes a self-fulfilling prophecy. So, in a sense, luck absolutely does exist.

My oldest daughter Wendy was busy with school, finishing up a degree in Russian and Political Science, and she had no time for dating. She was done with men, done with romance, dead male bodies strewn all over the campus of the University of Utah. One evening while she was setting fire to Atlanta, we joined friends for dinner. The ladies thought our waiter was handsome and thought he needed to meet Wendy the Hun. We showed the waiter a picture, and he agreed to call her. He did. It took a while to realize they were both in love, but it worked out. They've been married for 25 years.

What a lucky thing that we were there, that night, that moment, that waiter, as if it was meant to be. We randomly selected that night, made a last-minute decision where to eat, and here was mister right. The stars aligned that night.

Bull pucky. None of this was chance, or luck, or the stars aligning. An opportunity arose, we jumped on it. We made luck happen. We seized the moment.

After studying people who consider themselves lucky or unlucky, scientists have found that the "lucky" ones maximize chance opportunities and dare to follow their intuition to grasp those moments.

A *Wall Street Journal* article noted: If you are relaxed and happy, your world view becomes bigger, and you see more opportunities. If you're a flexible person, when those opportunities come in, you'll make the most of them.

Luck, coincidence, fate, destiny, the hand of god, whatever your personal beliefs, know this: you can actually control things more than you think. We can retrain our brains, rewire them to be open to opportunities, open to new experiences. Experts agree on this. Consider gratitude for example. When we think about our good fortune, when we express gratitude, when we live a grateful life, we create in our brain, a grateful neural pathway in our brain that becomes part of our lives. We've trained the brain, rewired the cerebellum to live a grateful life.

Here's Professor Hurst:

We become what we think we can become.

We are happier because when we tell our mind we are happier. Our mind rewards us with feelings of happiness and joy, and whether you're living a happy moment or just thinking about one, it is the same. Your brain knows no difference because you've trained it that way.

We become confident because we have taught our brain, trained it to feel confident, and so we step out, step off, step forward with more courage than we've ever known, slay the demons we have known far too well, far too long.

And we breathe again.

We celebrate our lives again.

We celebrate our passions again.

We fall in love again.

We make bigger, stronger, more lasting connections with our loved ones and friends, all of whom welcome you back from the precipice of doubt.Armed with this new knowledge, finally, we become converts to the church of Luck, the gospel of coincidence, the power of chance, taking chances, believing that chance, luck, serendipity are all things we can control.

We make our own luck.

Neither God nor other unseen forces in the universe have a finger on our lives, like some pawn in a chess game. We make our own moves. We are in charge of the board. And you can become a master of the game.You are an architect, you are an engineer, you are an electrician, you are a steelworker, a welder, a carpenter, and you have all the skills, all the tools you need to build your personal house of joy, the home where you belong.

Believe in luck. You can make it, and you can make it work for you. And now others will look at you, and they will envy you, and every person you meet, every time you walk down a busy street, someone will pause, and say to anyone who may be listening, "That is one very lucky girl."

"IT'S HARD TO DETECT LUCK. IT LOOKS SO MUCH LIKE SOMETHING YOU'VE EARNED."

FRANK A. CLARK

18
BUILDING FENCES

"Something there is that doesn't love a wall."

his is the opening line of **The Mending Wall**, a poem by Robert Frost. I think it's one of his most profound pieces, certainly his most approachable. I opened my book of his collected works, re-read this poem for the one-hundredth time, and had a few thoughts come to me about fences and walls.

I became a first-time homeowner at just about eight years into our marriage. Moving our very young family into a brand-new home was thrilling. The kids danced around, barefoot, on the new carpet, and ran from room to room, exploring every square inch of space. They loved it. I fretted endlessly about paying the mortgage.

I recalled signing about a thousand documents at the bank. When we finished, the woman who had handled all the details brought us some thank-you gifts. The two fancy pens we used to sign the documents, a couple of nice coffee mugs, a faux-leather binder to hold our copies of the paperwork, and, for my wife and I, one each ball and chain, carried in by a very large man who secured them to our ankles.

I had a hard time driving home from the bank with this new apparatus on my leg. Jill looked at me and said, "Did we really agree to drag this around for thirty years?"

We made the move and slowly began to settle. While Jill made curtains for the bedrooms and set about putting the feminine touch on furniture and décor, I had two important, mandatory, outside projects to attend to. First, sprinklers. You can't live in suburbia without a green lawn, and you can't have a proper green lawn without sprinklers.

The Book of Rules keeps growing.

Second, build a fence. I don't know which end of a hammer to use, I didn't own a saw, or a level, or a screwdriver, and I've never mixed cement nor set posts. "Can't we do without a fence?" I wondered. "Why does everyone put up a fence the minute they move in? Why can't it be open, flowing, more natural looking like Northern Virginia where we lived, or Atlanta whose suburban neighborhoods don't allow fencing?"

The answer is "Everyone builds a fence. That's just what we do."

More from the Robert Frost poem:

"On one side it comes to little more:

There where it is we do not need the wall:

He is all pine, and I am apple orchard.

My apple trees will never get across

And eat the cones under his pines, I tell him.

He only says, "Good fences make good neighbors."

I acquiesced and set about building a fence of rough-cut cedar and watched the rolling hills at the base of the Wasatch Mountain range transformed, overnight, from its natural beauty to a chopped up maze, a mélange of cedar, vinyl, stones, corrugated metal, and just about anything the young, new homeowners, burdened by the crushing debt of the Carter presidency, could find to build a fence.

More from the poem.

"Why do they make good neighbors? Isn't it

Where there are cows? But there are no cows.

128

Before I built a wall, I'd ask to know
What I was walling in or walling out,
And to whom I was like to give offense.
Something there is that doesn't like a wall,
That wants it down.

From the window in my den where I sit and write each morning, I can see thousands of acres of alfalfa, barley, oats, with not a fence in sight. Except where there are cows.

We lived in suburban neighborhoods for most of forty years. We raised our children in walkable neighborhoods, we enjoyed backyard barbeques and socials. We were a tight knit group, and it was not at all unusual when, on an evening walk, I smelled cookies baking in someone's oven. I followed my nose then pounded on the front door of the Lossers. When Rosalie opened the door I said, "I've come for a cookie." It was a very natural thing to do. She brought me some cookies, poured me a glass of milk, and we sat and talked for fifteen minutes.

Some of our closest, dearest friends, our deepest most enduring friendships, all came from those suburban years. Looking back on all of this, I am wondering, more than ever before, "Why did we all build fences?"

The wise poet closes with this:

"He will not go behind his father's saying,
And he likes having thought of it so well
He says again, "Good fences make good neighbors."

We are grateful we figured out a way to retire to farm country for a change of pace and a change of scenery. We love the open spaces.

I began thinking about fences in a new way after watching a reality TV show about a married couple in England who leave the big city and attempt to become farmers. Nothing goes right.

The sheep are unmanageable and regularly tear down fences. Wild animals are killing the chickens. The local zoning board won't allow them to build a small general store where neighbors would be able to buy fresh vegetables and cheese. The would-be farmer can't figure out how to run the new high-tech tractors, and he can't plow a straight line. At the end of the first full year, after investing about a half a million dollars, his net profit was around a hundred bucks.

Near the end of the series this struggling chap is asked to host the National Hedgelaying competition. People come from all over the UK for a chance to win $500 and a plaque. But it's much more than a plaque. It helps call attention to the pressing need of preserving a very important part of the British identity: Hedgerows.

They are essentially fences, but they are alive, growing, cleaning the air. With half a million miles of hedgerows in the UK, you don't have to go far to spot one.

Hedgerows come in a variety of shapes and sizes and can include many different species. Rural hedges are often a mix of shrub and tree species, such as hawthorn, blackthorn, hazel, ash, and oak. In more urban and landscaped settings, they are likely to include species like boxwood, yew, privet, and holly. (Quick note: Yew shrubs, "taxus bacatta," are a great choice. They are very dark green, and they have a unique texture, needle-like leaves which grow in two rows along a twig, similar to evergreens. They are regularly trimmed and hauled away for free by biomedical firms who have discovered medicinal qualities that are used in the fight against cancer. That's a good choice for a hedge.)Saving hedgerows is serious business. I found this alarming news on the web site of the National Hedgelaying Society, the NHS.

"Hedge numbers have declined rapidly in the last century. Around 118,000 miles of hedgerows have disappeared since 1950, due largely to intensification of agriculture. The loss has slowed since the 1990s, but neglect, damage and removal remain significant threats."

Hedge laying begins by clearing out all the overgrowth along the road or the edge of a farmer's field, leaving, for instance, new hazel shoots, probably six to eight feet in length. The professionals take a hatchet or machete, or an adze, (A really great Scrabble word) and cut the shoots nearly off, leaving just an inch or so of connection at ground level. The experts lay the shoots nearly parallel to the ground, then follow the edge of the property for a few acres or more, shaping the shoots into a work of art, looking for all the world like a woven basket. It's a hedge. It's a fence. It's a planet saving, ecofriendly masterpiece.

And it's alive.

Almost immediately the individual shoots begin re-blooming, and, after a time, the entire skeletal structure is covered with blossoms and leaves, and for the next two-hundred years, give or take, this will be a living, powerful weapon in the arsenal we deploy to help solve eco-challenges we face as earthlings. It's a remarkable thing I've not seen before.

Fences, all sorts of fences, walling in and walling out, have been on my mind of late. Not just structures of wood, wrought iron and stone, but rather the challenges and detours I'm constantly facing: These are the fences that stand in my way. And, my mind is swirling about some underdeveloped ideas I have about building "Living Fences."

I've started making a list of personal fences, brain fences, that I have built, the fences others have erected without consulting me, and the ones I have been trying diligently to tear down.

I have always shut people out, the largest of my personal fences, erected years ago, because I'm uncomfortable around those who are not like me, who don't measure up to my lofty standards and ignored this advice: *"Listen to others, even the dull and the ignorant. They too have their story"* (from **Desiderata)**.

This I call the "fence of arrogance." I can't begin to count individuals, outside my fence, who may have become close friends if I'd been a little more welcoming.

I have turned my attention to the "fence of condescension," keeping away all those individuals whom I have adjudged to have boring thoughts and worthless contributions to my life.

A young woman spoke to me recently about her fifteen-year battle with anxiety and depression, and her desperate struggle to reconnect with those who literally threw her in a ditch. Some of the most important people in her life have built impenetrable concrete walls keeping her locked in a prison, surrounded by razor wire atop a "fence of low self-worth."

I have listened to a new friend who has taken all the blame for the heartache and the unending sorrow of a broken relationship. Her fences won't allow her to share the blame. "This is the fence of "Let it go."

I've found a curious little fence, called the "fence of sorrow," sometimes referred to as a "grieving fence." It's been lowered so you can finally get over it. Also, the "fence of forgiveness," a frail, thing, that with even the slightest breeze, will tip over and simply blow away. There is, in your life, no doubt, a "fence of regret," or two, or three, and they are well built, preventing you from clearing out all the garbage in your yard.

There is a "fence of hate" surrounding, in one form or another, every one of us. As you cling to hatred, your brain traps it all in and becomes permanently hard-wired to hate. That's a fence that must go. There are "fences of fear," "fences of reluctance," "fences of shame," "fences of not me," that allow you to place blame and escape accountability. They are strong, and they are tall, and they are firm, and they are designed and built to hold us back and keep us from so many opportunities to learn and grow and progress. These fences are invisible to the untrained eye, making it easier for us to deny they exist.

You have a "fence of stubbornness, right? Admit it. Tear it down immediately and let others see a new, open minded, reborn person, ready to take new steps into the unknown.
There are two additional fences that can't be described any better than this:

"Envy, that other pernicious prescription for pulling you down and holding you back, is a sure way to devolve into desolation and isolation. With envy comes grudges, and the longer we hold grudges, the heavier they get."   P.K. Thomajan

You may have a fence in your mind that has not yet allowed you to fully comprehend the natural tendency you have to repeat, ad nauseum, the great lie, "I am not capable of love, I am unworthy of love, I am worthless," and you may spend the rest of your life believing this because your brain has jumped into the cruel choir of contradictions, creating noisy dissonance that constantly reminds you, like some drip, drip, drip in a torture chamber, you are worthless. After a time, you give up.

You've canceled your search for joy and have built a "fence of hopelessness." It has several different styles, the "fence of despair," the "fence of pity," and the very popular "fence of constant sorrow."

But there is also a "visceral fence" that lights up like Christmas, when you are taught and begin to internalize the mantra "I can be happy, I am entitled to joy, and I can live a joyous life." Just like Joshua who fought the battle of Jericho, horns will sound, fences and walls and all manner of barriers will crumble, millstones around your neck will fall to the ground in pieces, and you'll follow only the signs and the milestones that lead you ever on to the true love and joy you need.

Very recently, as the result of an emergency health event, I got very familiar with my "fence of pride," built for walling out. It's not like any traditional fence where you can walk up and peer through the wrought iron rods.

For me this was less like a fence, more like a tangle of chains that bound me and threw me to the ground, twisted me and tied me in a ball of knots and fear. I am now accepting more advice, more counsel, listening more to the loving voices around me, accepting help with my challenges, and I gladly accept every loaf of bread and every chocolate chip cookie brought to me by kind neighbors. My pride fence is down, and piece by piece it's being hauled away. No more walling out. In its place I am building a new "fence of humility," the perfect example of "walling in."

While dealing with a massive millstone of misery, a painful Parkinson's by-product, my perspective of almost everything has changed, my fences are coming down, and I am moving on.

There is valid scientific evidence in the field of neruoscience that demonstrates how repetitive learning—telling yourself over and over again that you can be healed—you can be happy. The neurons in your brain twist together to form a single, stronger **hardwired** strand.

You can hardwire your brain for happiness.

You can hardwire your brain for joy.

It's possible. It's a real thing.

Join me in my natural disdain for fences and my newfound fondness for tearing them down.

"SOMETHING THERE IS THAT DOESN'T LOVE A WALL, THAT WANTS IT DOWN."

ROBERT FROST

19
FIX IT IN POST

repaired a fence last spring. Record snowfall wreaked havoc on everything. Dug a hole, mixed a bag of cement and **set the post**.

Because I'm weird and curious, I like learning about words and their origins. So while I was out digging my hole in the impossibly rocky soil I sort of, kinda, fixated on the word, "post."

It comes from the Latin word post, no surprise, meaning "after," or "behind").

It turns out there are a bunch of different uses of this word.

In basketball, you run certain plays "down in the post," or you post up a guy meaning you back him down, push him out of the way. It helps if you have a large butt. (See Charles Barkley.)

You write a letter then post it. We don't write letters very much anymore, but we do create blog posts, and share them with our followers on social media.

A guard or a soldier stands his post at the gate. He is also a sentry. This is often used in the context of loyalty.

"Go to post" is a horse-racing term, meaning they are getting ready to start the race. So in some cases "post" means in the past but it can also refer to a beginning. I'm confused.

"Post" is used elsewhere in sports, signifying a victory or setting a record. "Tiger Woods posted a record 63 at the Masters Tournament."

Martin Luther posted his reformation thesis on the door of Castle Church in Wittenberg, Germany. In this context it means hanging something up in public.

"Post" is the name of the company that makes most of the cereal I eat. *Fruity Pebbles, Cocoa Pebbles, Raisin Bran.*

"Post" is tied up with the whole business of mailing a letter. In the U.S it is the post office, in the UK it is simply the post.

We have the *Washington Post*, a major newspaper, its name derived from the definition above of a posting of a notice.

A position of paid employment. "He resigned his post."

A general store at a military base is sometimes called the post. Also in the military you are assigned to an outpost in some faraway place.

Wiley Post was the first man to fly solo around the world. (I wonder if he ever had a bowl of *Post Toasties* on any of his flights?)

I've heard an epithet, "Dumb as a post," similar to dumb as a board, or dumb as a sack of hammers. I've got to tell you that many authors of blog posts sound dumb as a post.

Writer and columnist Emily Post was an arbiter of social etiquette and was the last word on manners. (She probably wouldn't have condoned serving a bowl of Post Cocoa Pebbles at a dinner party.)

The corporation **3M** invented *Post-It Notes*, those sticky little multicolored slips we place on our mirrors, our desks, and the entire periphery of our computer screens as reminders of tasks and appointments even though our handy phones now do the same thing.

Here's a new one you may not have seen:

"Can we fix this in post?"

Here's a quick background on its usage. It basically comes from Hollywood. In the business of making movies, or in my case thirty and sixty second television commercials we go through three phases:

First is **Pre-Production**. This is a meeting, a planning session, a time to organize and get everyone on the same page. It includes scouting a location, auditioning actors, hiring a director, writing and approving the script, and setting budget parameters. It can be tedious.

This is also the phase where we set goals and expectations, agree on timing for hitting a deadline, and where we listen to ideas and constructive input in order to get the story/message, and all the details exactly right.

Second, we go into **Production**. Cameras are on site, the lights are set, the actors are wired for sound and the director starts shouting, "Quiet on the set," and then, at long last, "Action."

I've been fortunate enough, or I have lived long enough, to have worked in production in both the old 35mm and 16mm film era, as well as the digital world. Digital is so easy compared to film. I'm exaggerating, but a digital camera is pretty much point and shoot.

With film we would have an assistant director who was adept at reloading film for the camera in the back of van, a portable dark room, going only by touch so as to prevent any light from ruining the film. With digital cameras there is no film or dark room. When using the old film technology and after eight or ten takes of a scene, and the director is happy, he calls out "check the gate." This means looking for hair or dust that may have been caught in the camera, leaving annoying, bouncy, dancing detritus in every shot.

A digital camera has no gate.

It was a painfully slow process, shooting on film, but it was always exciting to bring a story to life.

Phase Three: **Post Production.**

After a successful shoot there are still dozens of details to attend to. It begins with sending the film off to a lab, then sitting there for six or eight hours in color correcting.

Next, **Editing**. Originally, film editing was done on a flat bed, and the editors were kind of like a good tailor, cutting and piecing together each scene into a coherent finished product. Later it was possible to transfer the film to video and we could go into an edit bay and do final cut on computers.

Then comes sound design, music, effects, tweaking and mixing.

The final hurdle, convincing the client that the finished product was well worth busting the budget by 40%.

So many times, when we were on location, things weren't going well, and we couldn't get the right shot, someone would invariably ask, "can we fix it in post?" This meant "Can we change it in the edit room?" The answer is always no. When film is in the can, it's in the can, done, light burned into negatives. That's it.

Unless you have a major budget for special effects, "Postproduction" pretty much means pulling things together, not making changes. The sure way to successful postproduction is to have a killer pre-production plan. And the very best way to handle this complex task is to hire the very best people, masters of the craft.

I was always better at running the business, schmoozing clients, poaching good talent, leaving the creativity to the talented people I just poached.

We were in the business of storytelling. You are in the business of storytelling. You are living your story. You're writing your story. You're in control of your story. You are the author of both conflict and resolution. You are dealing with villains and heroes, mysteries, tragedies, comedy, character development, and happy endings.

The best way to tell your story is with very good pre-production planning. You don't get to choose where you are born, your environment or your parents. You don't even get to choose your own name. These are all elements over which you have no control. But you can control so much of the rest of your story. You are the author and the director. Your story begins now. What will it be?

You can control the people who have hurt you: Just write them out of the script. You can choose what to put into your brain and control your thoughts and actions. You have the power to kill off villains, run to the arms of heroes, decide what a hero is, find new heroes, find new relationships, re-build old friendships and be firmly in control of you.

There are going to be moments when you feel like you are in a dark room, blindly getting ready for the next shot. You may feel like you have a thousand pieces of film hanging on your wall and you are overcome with frustration trying to piece them together. Your sound design may be cluttered with too many voices telling you too many things, pulling you in too many directions, believing your life is nothing but chaos, confusion, and discombobulation.

And you can't fix things in post, meaning you can't do anything about the past. It's done. Move on.

Here's a title for your story:

"The End of Discombobulation."

There's a pretty good chance that no one in Hollywood options your script. You're probably not going to win an Academy Award. There's a chance no one will even read your story or watch your movie. Doesn't matter. You wrote it and learned what a powerful thing it can be to make a plan that's right for you, then execute on the plan with alacrity. Then, when the final credits roll, you'll see, up on the screen: "Original story by you. Executive Producer, you. Director, you.

"Quiet on the set. And…….Action!"

"THE HARDEST PART
OF MAKING A FILM IS
PUNCHING ALL THOSE LITTLE
HOLES ALONG THE SIDE."
GROUCHO MARX

20
HUMMINGBIRDS CLOSE-UP

On a recent Sunday afternoon, we joined with a group of 12 family members for dinner in the mountains. My wife's siblings and their spouses gathered to honor a sister-in-law who has very recently been going through chemotherapy to eradicate an enormous lymphoma that was crushing her internal organs. She was in great spirits, and we all drew strength from her rosy outlook.

We finished dinner but didn't move from the table for the next three hours. It's hard to get this group together on a regular basis so there was a lot of catching up to do. Eventually, we took our chairs out to the balcony where we continued to munch on forbidden sweet treats and set the summer sun.

Hummingbirds had been hanging around most of the afternoon, even though at this seven-thousand-foot mountain retreat the wildflowers were already gone, leaving these delicate birds with a depleted source of nectar. Purple blossoms on the alfalfa may have been enough reason for them to stay, but the bird feeders sitting on the balcony rail, for now, brought them around for our afternoon entertainment.

The party abruptly ended when we agreed it was time to call the hummingbird police. They were slow to arrive, but we had carefully taped off the crime scene to preserve any evidence. An investigation got underway.

It looked as though the sugary water in the red plastic feeder may have been poisoned. Directly below the feeder was a dead ruby-throated hummingbird. Inspector Poirot set about interrogating each one of us for clues and information.

The investigation is ongoing.

Sad as it was, it gave us a chance to see the little creature up close, its coloration, the length of its beak, things you never see on a humming bird because they never stop moving.

The detectives finally allowed us to leave, and as I pulled into my garage, I recalled, proudly, how I had, at various times over the years, personally saved the lives of three different hummingbirds right here in my garage.

On three different occasions a hummingbird would fly into my garage, flit around, and somehow get stuck in there because it couldn't figure out how to leave. This makes them sound stupid. But they are remarkably smart.

The human brain is about two percent of our body weight; a hummingbird's is double that. Their resting heartbeat is 225 beats per minute, 1,200 BPM in flight. On average they live about five years, and during that span they are a highly effective pollinator. They migrate to warmer climes to escape winter and go into a deep sleep called a torpor. This is like a bear that hibernates for the winter. Springtime, they return to the place where they were born, remembering along the way the exact migration route, and every flower they've visited.

The females build tiny, intricate nests made up of small bits of twigs and grass, held together by spider web threads they steal, expanding as babies hatch and grow. They are ingenious, clever, and highly efficient at their job.

(As I learned more details about these tiny creatures, I couldn't help wondering how scientists got a heart monitor strapped to the fragile frame, or how they measured the brain as a percent of body weight. Or how they count the number of times their wings flap in one second. I'll leave that to the experts.)

But, here he is, trapped in my garage, unable to see just below and behind him, three very large garage door openings, with sun streaming in them. Pretty hard to miss this obvious escape route. He keeps flying up, again and again, up, up, up, each time hitting the ceiling. He gets visibly tired and occasionally takes a brief rest. Out in the wild he must drink nectar all day to fuel his metabolism, and he may not have had a single drop in the last couple of hours while trapped in my garage.

He is exhausted now, desperate for a drink. He is panic stricken and can't think clearly, can't see the open doors. He keeps flying up, the way he would in his natural habitat, getting high above any predators. Up, up, up, crashing each time into the ceiling.

He is capable of flying up, down, forward, and backward, changing directions adroitly, in the blink of an eye, unlike any other bird on the planet. Despite his skills, despite his cleverness, he is gripped by fear. At this moment, his instincts are failing him in his desperate efforts to be free. His pre-programmed brain keeps sending him up, blind to the summer sunlight streaming through all three open doors, each one 9'x9.'

He can't see the light.

I grab a broom, swatting at him, never intent on killing him but trying in vain to gently force him down from the ceiling. No luck.

There is a large bin in the garage, filled with toys for our grandchildren and I notice three, bright yellow butterfly nets with plastic handles. They've been around for many years and the kids catch butterflies by the dozen, putting them in mason jars, watching them for a time, then releasing them. I put duct tape around one of the nets, then attached it to a plastic, extendable window cleaning rod. It reaches up to the ceiling and after just a few attempts I have the bird in my net. He didn't fight me, didn't try to evade me. It felt to me like he knew I was his rescuer, too dumb to fly out large open doors, but smart enough to discern my intent.

I still have the contraption I invented, stored safely in the corner of my garage, at the ready to save the next trapped hummingbird. Three lives saved and counting.

Up, up, up, banging into ceilings. This is a very human thing to do, don't you think. Our culture, our economy, our well-being, seems to revolve around the quest to be the best, everyone moving up. I've got to have a promotion in my company. I must have a bigger salary. I must have a new, luxury car. I have to move to a better neighborhood. I have to build a larger home. I have to dress in the latest fashion. Every time there is a new version of our cell phones with exciting features, we must upgrade immediately. One must not be seen with an outdated phone.

Up, up, up.

We are a culture of ladder climbers. Especially in developed nations. This is not universally true in all countries around the globe where tribal cultures find happiness and contentment in their unhurried, laid-back ways. But I've seen it in my world. In my tribe. I've lived it. I am complicit with the manufacturers of the ladders.

The drive to keep improving is a good thing. Make no mistake, I'm a firm believer that competition is a good thing. For instance, there was an all-out war between Marconi and Tesla to patent the high-frequency coil technology that gave us the radio.

The Wright brothers get credit for the first manned flight, but competition had been raging for years with teams all over the world trying to be the first to fly.

Idaho native Philo Farnsworth likely invented television, but many other competitors got the credit and the patents.

Competition is great for business and de rigueur for those who challenge the norm and find ways to make life better for everyone on the planet.

Chasing dreams is a good thing. Dream big, draw strength from "possibility nectar."

Climbing the corporate ladder is a good thing when we set our sights on growth and opportunity. Hundreds, thousands of people around the globe may benefit from our ambition, our drive.

Corporate ladder climbing is a bad thing when we resort to pulling the leg of the guy on the rung above us, dragging him down, stepping on his head to get to the top ahead of him. Ladder climbing is bad when we use lies, deceit, deception and back-room backstabbing to make oneself look good at someone else's expense. I came across an article authored by Tim Denning, a self-proclaimed personal development coach and writer. He is terrific. This is the headline of the article:

"I stopped climbing the corporate ladder when I realized everyone at the top was deeply unhappy."

I had to read it immediately. It's great.

Tim concludes the article by telling us, "It is good to climb the corporate ladder for a bit—especially when you are young and in need of valuable business skills. The key is not to get trapped, shackled, and muzzled. Once you play the game for too long, your imagination and creativity become so incapacitated it's hard to reignite them again. The corporate ladder won't make you happy. Find work that makes you come alive and helps make a difference. That's the holy grail." (Find Tim's insightful advice at www.timdenning.com)

On your desperate climb to the top, like the hummingbird who keeps hitting the ceiling, going up, up, always up, you may end up overworked, over stressed, over-heated, over-loaded, over-burdened and, along with your high expectations you have high blood pressure. Along with your ambition you have, anxiety, angina, bleeding ulcers, sleepless nights, crushing stress, migraines, and other maladies that beset even the best.

But hey, you are at the top. You did it. Congratulations. You are a daring doer, admired by those around you. Enjoy the view from the top but be cautious. Just below you there is a gaggle of greedy goons, ready, in an instant to pull on your leg and knock you off the ladder. They are very good at it because you showed them how it is done.

The case of the ruby throated hummingbird, the strange death of even one of these mini marvels seemed to create a momentary tear in the fabric of time. It was easy to say that it was just one bird, there are millions more. But our family of mostly septuagenarians, on the balcony that summer evening, overlooking endless fields of alfalfa, setting the sun in the thin air of the mountains of northern Utah, we took a collective breath and a private pause. We are aging, we have failing health, we have any number of family, physical, and emotional challenges, but for now we are cheering on to victory a sister, mother, and wife who is not going to let cancer trap her in a garage. She is going to follow the light and get back to her wonderfully rich life as a music teacher, a loving grandmother, and a firm believer in the power of **"UP."**

The Author

I'm a retired ad guy, brand strategist,
and palm reader. The brand guy decides what
story to tell, the ad guy finds a clever way to tell
it, and the palm reader, well no one in the ad
business really knows what they're doing,
so we spend a lot of time pretending we
know more than the client.

I have published one novel, a work of historic fiction
about sheep shearing, and three non-fiction books,
each filled with quirky observations about skunks,
Kirby vacuum cleaner salesmen, boy scout merit
badges, penguin poop in the Antarctic, and a wild
man from Borneo with a bone in his nose.

From the mind of a simple man, each book is a collection
of simple tales and the big lessons they taught me.

Mark Hurst

PRESERVATION BOOK
SOUTH JORDAN, UT 84009
PRESERVATIONBOOKS.COM

Made in the USA
Columbia, SC
27 July 2024

39448436R00090